DISTANT SHORES

Pages From Newfoundland's Past

Calvin Coish

LIFESTYLE BOOKS
1994

LIFESTYLE BOOKS
6 Dawe Crescent
Grand Falls-Windsor, NF
A2A 2T2

© 1994 Calvin Coish

ALL RIGHTS RESERVED. No part of this work may be reproduced in any form or by any means without the prior written permission of the publisher or author. Any request for photocopying, recording, taping, or information storage and retrieval of any part of this book shall be directed in writing to the Canadian Reprography Collective, 379 Adelaide Street West, Suite M1, Toronto, ON M5V 1S5

Cover Photo: Newfoundland Scene by K. Bruce Lane

Canadian Cataloguing in Publication Data
  Coish, E. Calvin, 1948-

   Distant shores

   ISBN 0-9691126-2-9

   1. Newfoundland – History. I. Title

   FC2161.C64 1993   971.8   C93–098705-5
   F1122.C64 1993

Printed and bound in Newfoundland

TABLE OF CONTENTS

THE NEWFOUNDLAND COASTAL BOATS: Vital Link	1
BONAVISTA: Historic Landfall	8
NEWFOUNDLAND FOLK MEDICINE:	
Molasses, Myrrh And Maggots	14
CUPIDS: Newfoundland's Valentine Town	21
PRINCESS PAMELA: Lady From Fogo	26
GRAND BANK: Child Of The Sea	32
NEWFOUNDLAND'S PUGILISTS: Punching It Out	37
SIGNAL HILL: Sentinel Of History	42
FISHING ON THE LABRADOR: Good Times And Bad	49
GREENSPOND: Outport Legacy	55
TREPASSEY: River Of Roses	61
NEWFOUNDLAND SHIPWRECKS: The Way Of The Sea	66
PLACENTIA: More Than A Pleasant Place	72
CARBONEAR: Newfoundland's Gibraltar	79
NEWFOUNDLAND: Trans-Atlantic Stepping Stone	85
FERRYLAND: Baltimore's Place	93
NEWFOUNDLAND'S PIRATES:	
The Jolly Roger And Pieces Of Eight	100
L'ANSE-AUX-MEADOWS: Shades Of The Vikings	107
THE PORTUGUESE IN NEWFOUNDLAND:	
Adventure In Their Blood	113
TWILLINGATE: A Tale Of Two Islands	118
RED BAY: Basking In History	125
BRIGUS: A Glorious Past	131
THE EATON'S CATALOGUE: A Newfoundland Tradition	138
TRINITY: Living History	145
FOGO ISLAND: Still Lots Of Fire	151
HARBOUR GRACE: Pirate's Hangout	156
CATALINA AND PORT UNION: Old And New	162
THE NEWFOUNDLAND RAILWAY: Gone But Not Forgotten	168
THE COLONIAL BUILDING: If These Walls Could Talk	175
BURIN: Between Past And Present	183

ACKNOWLEDGEMENTS

The selections in this volume are based on articles published in *The Atlantic Advocate*, which was a part of the life of Atlantic Canadians for many years. For their support and encouragement of my writing efforts, I wish to thank the editors of that fine magazine, especially Jim Morrison, Hal Wood and Dawn Haines. To readers who have written or phoned with their comments, questions and requests concerning my writings, I also express my appreciation.

My sincere thanks also to the staff of the Harmsworth Library in Grand Falls-Windsor and the Newfoundland Historical Society, in particular the late Bobbie Robertson, to whom this book is dedicated. I also wish to thank the staff of the Newfoundland Department of Development who, over the years, provided many illustrations to accompany my articles. Worthy of special mention are Jack Byrne and Wayne Sturge of that Department. My thanks also to A. R. Scammell, Gary Saunders, the late J. R. Smallwood and others for offering words of encouragement.

Calvin Coish
Grand Falls-Windsor, Nfld.
November 1993

THE NEWFOUNDLAND COASTAL BOATS: Vital Link

"The steamer's coming! The steamer's coming! I remember hearing that familiar shout many times as a boy on Fogo Island, for the steamer - as we called the coastal boat - was our lifeline to the outside world. It brought letters and parcels and husbands and fathers returning home after a fall of back-breaking labour on the mainland or in the "lumber woods".

I remember too the terrifying brrmp! brrmp! of the steamer's sonorous horn, as the impressive black ship with white trim hove too just inside the mouth of the harbour. There was something awesome too about the crew members decked off in their smart outfits and the captain, often sporting a thick beard, wearing his distinctive black and white cap. For years in our community there was no wharf in water deep enough to accommodate the draft of the coastal boats, so the steamer would drop anchor just inside the mouth of the harbour and lower the gangplank. Then the punts and skiffs would converge on the huge ship, eager to deliver or pick up mail and freight and passengers. When they built a government wharf so that ships could tie up there, some of the romance of the steamers was lost. I remember in 1959 my father's first car being hoisted off the deck of the Avalon Trader onto the government wharf in the middle of the night.

I remember also listening to CBC Radio many times and hearing the shipping report: "The Glencoe enroute to Lewisporte; the Bonavista at St. John's, loading for ports to Nain." Some years later, as I was spending a summer on a tiny island off the coast of Labrador, the arrival of the Bonavista off Pack's Harbour with mail and freight and passengers generated at least a touch of the same excitement the steamer brought to so many Newfoundland communities for so many years.

The Old Northern Ranger   CN Marine

The story of Newfoundland's coastal boats goes back to 1838, when the Newfoundland government offered five hundred pounds sterling to anyone who would set up a steamer service between St. John's and Nova Scotia. The following year, Governor Prescott asked the British government to make St. John's a port of call on the steamer route between England and America.

In 1840, the H.M.S. Spitfire, a British man-of-war, became the first steamer to appear in Newfoundland, when it sailed into St. John's harbour on November 5, carrying a detachment of the Royal Newfoundland Veteran Companies from either Halifax or Quebec. One observer described the Spitfire as "a sea monster breathing fire and smoke and thrashing the water into foam." That same year, the Nova Scotia government allocated 1500 pounds sterling to finance a steamer service to Newfoundland.

In 1842, two more steamers, the John McAdam, from Cork, Ireland and the St. George, from Liverpool, England, arrived in Newfoundland. On April 24, 1844, Newfoundland's first mail and passenger steamer, the North America, under the command of Captain Richard Meagher, arrived in St. John's, only two and a half days after sailing from Halifax, Nova Scotia. Around 1845, the Osprey provided a steamer service from St. John's to Bermuda, via Halifax.

In 1851, the Newfoundland legislature provided 1500 pounds sterling for a fledgling steamer service and brought in the Lady LeMarchant to carry mail and passengers between St. John's and various points in Conception Bay. Finding the ship too big, the government then brought in the 200-ton schooner-rigged Ellen Gisborne in 1853. The Lady LeMarchant and the Ellen Gisborne marked the real beginning of Newfoundland's coastal boat service. Later, the Victoria, a 254-ton propeller-driven steamer provided the first service to the south and northeast coasts. The ship, built and registered at Philadelphia, flew the Stars and Stripes, despite the objections of more than a few Newfoundlanders. Later still, other ships – the Ariel, the Curlew, the Plover – expanded the coastal service even further. In 1871, Labrador got its first steamer service, provided by off-duty sealing ships during the summer months.

But it was really Sir Robert Reid, builder of the Newfoundland Railway, who started Newfoundland's modern coastal boat service in the 1890s with the Alphabet Fleet. Nicknamed "Reid's Yachts", these vessels became known for their bowsprits, graceful

The Burin   CN Marine

hulls, flared cutwaters and clipper sterns. The first eight of these, all built in Scotland, bore distinctly Scottish names - Argyle, Bruce, Clyde, Dundee, Ethie, Fife, Glencoe, Home. Later came the Invermore, Kyle, Lintrose and Meigle. Each of these ships had a distinctive place in the Newfoundland marine transportation network. In 1899, the Glencoe, which had been built mainly to serve Labrador, was put on the St. John's to Halifax run. Later, as part of its impressive 57-year tenure, the ship served the southwest coast. The Ethie ran in Conception and Trinity Bays, while the Home and the Clyde served Notre Dame Bay.

The Kyle, one of the most famous of the old coastal boats, came on the scene in 1913, and was probably the first regular passenger ship assigned to the Labrador run. In her day, the Kyle was the epitome of elegance. A reporter at the time offered this description: "The state rooms are veritable miniature palaces. They contain from four to six berths and are painted dead white on the ceilings and the rest enamel white. Each room has its own wash basin, and a cunningly devised little ladder to take one to the top berth without the necessity of climbing up the lower berth. The ladies' cabin amidships is also an apartment fitted in the sumptuous way with mirrors set about, handsome furniture and cork and cloth carpets. The ship is well ventilated and lit throughout with electricity, as well as telephones." So important a place did the Kyle come to secure in Newfoundland's marine history that the magazine *Them Days* devoted a full issue to memories and impressions of the grand old ship. Today, the hulk of the Kyle lies beached near Harbour Grace. Despite numerous appeals to the government, nothing has been done to restore the majesty of this ship, which served Newfoundlanders so well for more than 50 years. A maritime museum would be a fitting fate for this once-proud vessel.

In a 1922 report to Robert Reid, R. C. Moran wrote that "a very great proportion of the traffic of the small population can be better handled by water than by rail and at much less expense."

After serving their purposes admirably in Newfoundland, many of the coastal boats went to second careers. For example, the Imperial Russian government purchased the Bruce, the Lintrose and four other ships for service on the White Sea. In September 1986, the Bonavista retired after 40 years of service, mainly on the run to Labrador. The Lake Melville Tourist Association wanted to turn the ship, which had won a place in the hearts of many Labradorians, into a tourist attraction, but a Quebec company purchased the venerable old vessel. Another coastal boat, the Petite Forte, went into service as a missionary boat in the West Indies.

Some ships of the Newfoundland coastal fleet came to more ignominious ends. The Fife was lost in the Strait of Belle Isle on November 14, 1900. On December 11, 1919, the S.S. Ethie ran aground at Martin's Point, near Bonne Bay; two weeks later, the Dundee came to grief on Grassy Island, near Carmanville.

Other names come to mind when rummaging through the legacy of the Newfoundland coastal boats – the Springdale and its sister ship, the Bar Haven, sister ships Burgeo and Baccalieu, the Hopedale (destroyed by fire in 1984), the Northern Ranger (replaced by a ship of the same name in October 1986). Marine Atlantic still operates coastal boats along the south coast and in Labrador, as well as the Sir Robert Bond, a ferry which carries passengers, freight and automobiles between the island

and Labrador.

Then there were the Clarenville Boats, nicknamed the Splinter Fleet, all constructed at the Clarenville Shipyard. These sturdy, wooden vessels were very much a part of the coastal boat heritage and carried the names of Newfoundland communities - Bonne Bay, Burin, Clarenville, Codroy, Exploits, Ferryland, Glenwood, Placentia, Trepassey, Twillingate. The first of these, the Clarenville, slid down the ways on July 12, 1944, after being christened by Lady Walwyn, the Governor's wife. Ships of the Splinter Fleet proved their worth time and time again in the cold reaches of the Arctic and Antarctic, and on the high seas all around the globe. More than one was pressed into service in the hunt for seals off the east coast of Canada. One member of the Splinter Fleet reportedly became a floating restaurant in Ontario.

Today, road and air traffic have largely taken over the once vital role of Newfoundland's coastal boat service. But it's still possible to book a trip on a coastal boat along the south coast or north to Labrador.

BONAVISTA:
Historic Landfall

It's an unpretentious, quiet fishing community with a population of around 5,000. Many historians contend it stands close to the original North American landfall of the Italian explorer John Cabot. The name of the town is virtually a household word across Canada and it's a rare Canadian indeed who hasn't hummed the familiar line: "From Bonavista to Vancouver Island."

The story goes that, on sighting land on or around June 24, 1497, Cabot or one of his crew shouted "Buona Vista," an Italian expression which translates roughly "O happy sight!" On the earliest maps the town was designated Buona Vista or Buena Vista. Over almost five centuries the name has been anglicized to Bonavista.

Despite its claim to fame as a cradle of white settlement in North America, Bonavista is still relatively unspoiled by twentieth-century technology and retains much of its historic and rustic appeal. The influence of the earliest explorers and settlers is still quite evident in areas of the town with names like Canaille (French) and Mockbeggar (English).

Records indicate the town of Bonavista was first settled by the British around 1600 and vied with St. John's, farther south along the east coast, in economic and cultural importance. In 1667 Bonavista was the second-largest community in Newfoundland, with 18 houses, compared with 45 in St. John's. By 1732, Bonavista was home to six per cent of the Newfoundland populace and was the most prosperous region on the island. The first school on the island (and the first Protestant school in Canada) was built there in 1726 for "all the poor people." In 1760 Captain James Cook made the town his home port during his exhaustive and incredibly accurate (even by today's standards) surveys of Newfoundland's northeast coast. In 1843, the 2,000 residents of Bonavista landed 40,000 seals.

Like many early North American settlements, Bonavista had a whipping post at which those who had committed even the most trifling crimes were flogged. One noted case was that of Joseph Batt, a member of Captain Cook's crew, who was tried and found guilty of pilfering a pair of shoes and buckles worth seven shillings and sixpence (about a dollar). Batt was sentenced to receive fifteen lashes at the post. A few days later, angry residents tore down the hated post. In spite of his brief flirt with notoriety, Joe Batt's name still lives on in Newfoundland. We are told that Batt deserted Cook's ship in Gander Bay and, from there, found his way to Fogo Island. To this day, one of the most unforgettable place names in the province is Joe Batt's Arm.

For two centuries or more, Bonavista was the chief port from which sealers and fishermen set out each spring. As early as the sixteenth century, Bonavista was a major port for European fishing fleets, and Basque fishermen used the town as a base for sealing and whaling operations.

So strategically important was Bonavista that it was quite often the scene of skirmishes and full-scale battles between the British settlers and French and Indian invaders. In the nine years from 1696 to 1705, Bonavista was attacked four times by the French and their Micmac allies. One of the most engaging stories involves the New Englander Michael Gill. The date was August 18, 1704 and the French had captured three boats in Bonavista harbour. Afraid of being taken prisoners, the settlers of Bonavista fled for the relative safety of the nearby woods. When the French tried to seize a fourth ship, this one captained by Gill, they were not so

Cape Bonavista Lighthouse Calvin Coish

successful. For six hours the two sides traded volleys. Frustrated, the French set fire to one of the captured ships and sent in drifting toward Gill's vessel. But Gill maneuvered his ship out of the path of the floating inferno. The French tried again with another burning ship. Again Gill steered his ship out of the way.

When the people who had taken to the woods saw Gill's determination and success, they came out of hiding. Overwhelmed at the sight of all those people, the French retreated.

The next year, however, the French again attacked Bonavista. This time, they captured the town, no doubt partly because Captain Gill was no longer there to defend it. As a matter of interest, Gill's oldest son became the first colonel of the Newfoundland militia, a younger son became chief magistrate of St. John's, and his grandson became a successful merchant.

One of the most visible and romantic links with Newfoundland's past is the lighthouse at Cape Bonavista, restored to its late-nineteenth-century condition some years ago. Built in 1843, the lighthouse is protected as a provincial historic site. Historians believe that much of the stone used to construct the lighthouse tower was brought in from Nova Scotia.

Bonavista has moved to strengthen its claim as Cabot's landing place. At the top of a barren, rocky hill stands a towering, bronze statue of the famed adventurer. The chemical action of salty spray carried by the ever-present wind has given the figure a blue-green hue. Still, there's something awe-inspiring, almost sacred, about standing at the base of the monument and gazing eastward across the limitless expanse of the Atlantic Ocean.

What is reportedly the oldest surviving house in Newfoundland is located at Bonavista. The house was built in 1811 by a Scot named Alexander Strathie for a prominent Bonavista merchant, William Alexander. Bridge House, as it is called, was used as a boarding house during the early 1900s.

The majestic old courthouse is still there on a hill overlooking the harbour, with its breakwater and piers. The courthouse was constructed in 1900 on the site of the 1704 battle involving Michael Gill. A plaque in front of the building commemorates Gill's heroism.

While Bonavista appears in no real danger of adopting the skyscraper mentality of much of urban North America, some of its old flavour is disappearing. The high, unpainted picket and paling fences are being pushed aside to make room for widened streets and increasingly familiar blacktop. The venerable old stone and concrete Christ Church, which had been slowly crumbling into ruin, has been levelled and replaced by a modern, much smaller building, which doesn't have quite the character of the old one.

Like most Canadian towns, Bonavista has its modern side – a town hall, a community college campus, a super-modern high school, new houses. The road leading into town has seen a proliferation of gas stations, takeouts, nightclubs and other commercial enterprises. Several new businesses have moved into the town. The old cottage hospital has been given a modern look.

Until the cod moratorium hit the province like a gale-force wind, the lifeblood of Bonavista was the fishery. Some years ago the government constructed a marine haulout and service centre there.

If you take the time – about an hour – to drive the length of the Bonavista Peninsula from Clarenville on the Trans-Canada Highway to Bonavista at the eastern tip, you'll catch a glimpse of the real, still largely undisturbed Newfoundland. Don't miss a chance to visit the Dungeon, near Cape Bonavista. No, it's not at all like the Tower of London, where many a head once rolled. The Dungeon consists of two huge, gaping holes which have been gouged through 200 feet of solid rock by the pounding sea. At low tide it's possible to row a boat through the tunnels into an inner pool. Who knows? Perhaps Cabot and his men stared in awe at this natural wonder. At any rate, making a trip to the place Cabot happened upon some five hundred years ago is something like making a pilgrimage to a very special place.

Statue of John Cabot at Cape Bonavista   Calvin Coish

NEWFOUNDLAND FOLK MEDICINE:
Molasses, Myrrh and Maggots

The folk medicine tradition in Newfoundland goes back many years to a time before the days of doctors, when people coped the best way they knew how with all kinds of ailments. Early settlers brought many of these traditions from their homelands – Ireland, England, Scotland, France. Other treatments had their origins among the native Indians and Eskimos. Still others came about when, of necessity, people devised concoctions and performed their own medical practices, using whatever happened to be handy – alder buds, bark, flour, myrrh, molasses, maggots, mud.

Early settlers generally managed to come up with some "remedy" for just about every illness they knew. Take boils, for example. To extract the core of a boil, a person would pour hot water into a bottle, then empty the bottle and place its mouth over the boil. As the bottle cooled, the core of the boil came out. Another remedy, somewhat less scientific perhaps, was to mix a bottle of flour water. The afflicted person would then, as one old-timer told me, "take a glutch every morning for nine mornings", then break the bottle. The cure seems to have worked, for, as the gentleman said, "I haven't had a boil since." Another rather unusual cure for boils required the person to drink a teaspoon of gunpowder mixed with a tablespoon of molasses.

In her intriguing book, *Our Life On Lear's Room Labrador*, Greta Hussey talks about "water whelps" or "water pups", a common curse of men who lived and worked at sea. These "pups" were painful boils which appeared on the wrists from the chafing of wet oilskins. Fishermen commonly wore chains on their wrists to prevent this ailment, but that precaution was not always successful.

A common treatment for "pups" (as well as for other boils) was to put a poultice made of molasses and flour or laundry soap and sugar on the boil to draw out the core. "It was discovered, more or less by accident," noted Hussey, "that if, when the boils first began to appear, the little yellow pustule was opened with a sterilized needle and a drop or two of Sloan's Liniment poured in, it really did the trick and cleared them up before they grew to cause trouble."

A curious assortment of other ingredients – egg white, powdered sea shells, burnt cream, dried alder buds mixed with tar, fousty (mouldy) bread, goose grease, even scorched cloth – went into the creation of various poultices. A common poultice, which I can remember my mother using, was a bread poultice (which consisted of stale bread soaked in boiling water) wrapped in cloth and put on a rising finger or other infected part of the body. Another poultice, used to treat sores or a dog bite, was made from the mulched, boiled inner bark of a juniper tree.

To stop bleeding, Newfoundlanders sometimes used turpentine from fir trees, mud, myrrh, molasses, flour, even cobwebs. To stop nosebleed, certain persons, known as "charmers", would recite a secret phrase or perform some mystical rite. One widely-used nosebleed cure required the victim to wear a green ribbon around the neck until the ribbon wore out.

Warts, the bugbear of many a Newfoundland youngster, were subjected to every imaginable form of torture and treatment. One practice was to rub a potato or piece of meat on the wart and bury the potato or meat. As the potato or meat decayed, the warts were supposed to disappear. Every community had at least one person reputed to have the ability to "put away" warts. Generally, the person possessing this magical power would take a look at the warts, count them, and then admonish the afflicted person not to look at the warts for so many days. Another approach was to count the warts and chalk the same number of marks on the back of a stove. As the chalk marks disappeared from the stove, so did the warts disappear from the person's body. Or, persons having warts on their hands might wrap as many pebbles as they had warts in a piece of rag and drop the little package on a road, where some unsuspecting person would pick it up, thus acquiring the other person's warts.

For that throbbing curse known as toothache, early Newfoundlanders came up with countless remedies. One treatment required the person with the aching tooth to hold a mouthful of vinegar as long as possible. Another cure was to collect pebbles from the grave of a religious person. There were also people in many communities who had a reputation for being able to "charm away toothache", generally by putting a finger on the offending area and reciting some special saying.

Then there was cod liver oil. How well I remember it, the unpalatable bane of my early schooldays. I had quite a distaste for the stuff, and, quite frankly, would go to almost any length to avoid consuming it. Once, after receiving a bottle of cod liver oil at school, I loosened the cap and slipped the bottle into my bookbag, along with assorted scribblers and textbooks. Upon arriving home, much to my parents' dismay (and my delight), I discovered (not quite to my surprise) that the entire contents of the bottle had dribbled among the contents of the bag. For the rest of that school year my books bore a distinctive yellowish cast and gave off the nauseating smell of the dreaded cod liver oil. Well-meaning parents struggled to convince us that cod liver oil could prevent colds and restore flagging levels of minerals and vitamins in the body. But I never for a moment believed that. Mind you, there were some youngsters who did believe that and who imbibed the slippery stuff until their inside shirts turned yellow. I might add that cod liver oil capsules are still popular with many Newfoundlanders. In fact, I myself have tried swallowing them, but, for some reason, perhaps related to my childhood experiences, they never make it past my tonsils.

Doctors and researchers may try to convince us that there is no cure for the common cold. Try telling that to a Newfoundlander and he's likely to laugh at you. Of course there's a cure for the cold! Or perhaps I should say there are a dozen cures, including boiled blackberry bushes, boiled Indian Tea (a low shrub), or a mixture of rum and mustard. To say nothing of extract of wild cherry, spirits of turpentine, snakeroot, and the ever-reliable Buckley's Mixture. I remember especially the warm, almost numbing sensation of camphorated oil – heated on the stove, then rubbed on the chest and back to fight a chest cold. Then a sheet of warm flannel, placed on the chest and tucked inside the pajamas, would continue the healing throughout the night. A salt herring, tied around the throat with a cloth, offered another rather unsavoury remedy for either a sore throat or mumps. Fortunately, I was never subjected to this particular "treatment".

Some Newfoundlanders resorted to making their own cough drops. The recipe called for molasses, a couple of drops of kerosene oil, two or three drops of Minard's Liniment, and a dash of pepper, all to be put in a dipper, placed on the stove and boiled until thick. The potion could then be dipped out with a spoon or, once cooled, cut into squares.

And how did Newfoundlanders fight indigestion in the days before Rolaids, Tums and Eno? Some used boiled bog beans, which look something like green beans. Rumour has it that, at times, some enterprising souls tossed in a few raisins among the bog beans to produce a kind of homemade brew. Others used spruce buds, alder buds, boiled ground juniper, or dogberry extract to settle a churning stomach.

Hussey cites the case of John "Bigger" Dyson, who was apparently dying of pneumonia. Hussey tells us that a Mrs. Coveyduck from Clarke's Beach fried onions in cod liver oil and placed them on Dyson's chest, changing poultices all night, until Dyson regained consciousness. Dyson recovered, and, when bothered with a stitch in his chest, used a few drops of Sloan's Liniment with a teaspoonful of sugar. A mustard poultice on the chest was also supposed to do the trick in combatting

FOLK MEDICINE

pneumonia.

Another time, Hussey's oldest sister Jessie came down with something called worm fever, a rather serious condition. The same Mrs. Coveyduck gathered some periwinkles from along the landwash, crushed them to a powder, mixed the powder with molasses, and gave the concoction to Jessie. She also gave the sick girl some of her own hair, cut up fine and mixed with molasses.

The standard cure for headache was (and still is for many Newfoundlanders) to tie a band of cloth tightly around the head. Walking backwards, around in a circle, is supposed to enhance the potency of this particular remedy.

To overcome the pain of rheumatism, some old-timers used a rather noxious potion of bottled, dissolved jellyfish. Wintergreen, rubbed lightly on the joints, was a more common treatment. My grandmother swore by Templeton's TRCs in coping with her own rheumatism.

Common remedies for hiccups included turning a cup upside down, drinking a glass of water quickly, or holding your breath as long as possible. And there were more drastic treatments, like giving the hiccuping person a sudden fright.

There were people who even had a trick for getting rid of tapeworms. The tapeworm carrier was told to fast for several hours. Then the victim had only to open his mouth over a saucer of evaporated milk which had just been boiled. The tapeworm would then appear in search of the milk.

The list of treatments and cures goes on and on. A pebble under the tongue was a certain cure for a pain in the side. To cure a hernia in a child, one had only to split a green witch hazel tree and shove the child through it. Hot tallow from a burning candle fixed ingrown toenails. Pine tar did the trick on hemorrhoids. The first snow of May, melted and boiled, offered soothing relief for sore eyes. A raisin hastened the healing of an infant's umbilical cord, while scorched flour served as powder for the baby's bottom. There was even a cure for sore lips – hatchet sweat people called it. To obtain this particular medication, one had merely to light a piece of cloth or paper wrapped around the blade of an axe. The grease produced, although it stung the lips, is said to have worked almost right away. Gunpowder horn scrapings steeped in hot water were effective in controlling urinary problems.

Then there were the countless brand name remedies, such as Spirits of Nitre (for fever), Brick's Tasteless (to restore lost appetite), Radway's Ready Relief (for stomach pains), Dr. Chase's Nerve Food Pills, and Dodd's Kidney Pills.

And just how do maggots fit into this? We've all heard how, in the days before antiseptics, maggots served as excellent disinfecting agents for wounds. The Eskimos must have known about this, for they used maggots in a poultice.

It is possible to come up with all kinds of plausible explanations for the success or reported success of many old-fashioned remedies, but the simple truth is that, for those self-sufficient early settlers, there were no other treatments. Either they used these or allowed an illness to take its course, which might well be deadly.

CUPIDS:
Newfoundland's Valentine Town

Legend tells us of a mythical character named Cupid out to shoot his arrows at the love-prone every February. Considering the wealth of intriguing and unusual place names peppering a map of Newfoundland, it's not really surprising that this province has a community named after the romantic little rascal. The little community of Cupids snuggles cozily into a sheltered harbour, flanked by gently sloping hills, on the western side of Conception Bay. Just across the neck of land is Brigus, home of the famed mariner and Arctic explorer Captain Bob Bartlett.

Back in 1610, the London and Bristol Company of Gentlemen Adventurers commissioned John Guy to set sail across the Atlantic to Newfoundland. Guy was to send back to England fish, oil, furs, hazel nuts and kelp, all intended to provide a handsome return for the company's shareholders. Fish, oil, furs and kelp Guy would find; hazel nuts he would not. When Guy and his brother-in-law William Colston settled here with thirty-nine other people in August of 1610, they reportedly named the place Cuper's Cove. Sir William Vaughan referred to the little village as Cupert's Cove, as did John Mason on his map of 1625. Other variations on the present name include Coopers Cove, Cubbitts Cove, and Cupperes Cove.

In that first unusually mild winter nearly four hundred years ago, the colonists built a mansion (which Guy christened "Sea Forest House"), a storehouse, grist-mill, sawmill, workhouse and stockade equipped with three cannon. The settlers also constructed six fishing boats and a twelve-ton shallop.

The following year Guy went back to England for a visit. When he returned to Cupids he brought Reverend Erasmus Stourton, the first Church of England clergyman

John Guy Monument  Nfld. Dept. of Development

to settle in Newfoundland.

In the first attempt to establish a central government in Newfoundland, the British government gave Guy wide-ranging powers to bring law and order to the colony. In a letter dated July 29, 1612, Guy reported that Peter Easton's pirate fleet was terrorizing fishing vessels and communities along the Newfoundland coast. Generally, Cupids seems to have escaped this harrassment, although one year Guy claimed that pirates stole goods worth 20,000 pounds from his colony. It seems that piracy was the reason Guy decided against setting up a colony farther south at Renews in 1612. Many Newfoundland communities, including Cupids, had fishermen who took to piracy on the high seas, earning a far better income than they could get from fishing.

To add substance to the assorted rumours which tend to proliferate concerning pirates and their escapades, there is at least one documented account of buried treasure being found at Cupids. Back in 1810, a Mrs. LeGrow unearthed a box of English and Spanish gold coins which had been buried in her garden.

While exploring the Newfoundland coast in the fall of 1612, Guy and his men came across a band of Beothuck Indians at Bull Arm and exchanged gifts for furs. This was reportedly the first meeting between English settlers and Beothucks. The winter of 1612 proved to be much harsher than the previous one, claiming eight of the colony's settlers and many animals.

On March 27, 1613, Nicholas Guy's wife gave birth to a baby boy, the first child of European ancestry born in Newfoundland, except for a Viking child born around 1,000 A. D. at L'Anse-aux-Meadows. A plaque presented to the town of Cupids in 1974 notes that event. A month later, John Guy, in conflict with his sponsors over profits, wages and property grants, returned to England, leaving his brother-in-law in charge of the colony.

Colston stayed on at Cupids until 1615, when he handed control of the settlement over to Captain John Mason, who took the job quite seriously, overseeing a fish business at Cupids and another at Bristol's Hope. Mason also surveyed the coastline, protected the settlers from pirates, and was the first governor to bring his wife to Newfoundland.

The Masons had as a servant an Indian named Squantum, who, along with nineteen other Indians, had been captured in New England in 1614 by Thomas Hunt, one of John Smith's captains, and taken to Malaga, where he was sold as a slave. John Mason's wife, Anne, taught Squantum to help her in the garden, to practice the Church of England religion, and to speak English. Squantum was later taken back to his home in New England. No doubt the Pilgrims were more than a little surprised when they stepped ashore at Plymouth Rock to meet an Indian who spoke fluent English.

After six years as governor of the colony, Mason went back to England and left Robert Hayman in charge. Mason later went on to establish a colony in what is now New Hampshire, Hayman stayed on as governor until 1628, but it seems that his sponsors back in England lost interest in this troublesome, unprofitable colony and, as historian M. F. Howley suggested, "the settlement gradually sank into insignificance before the newly rising settlement (Ferryland) to the south."

But, the community prospered again, for in 1836 it was home to 840 people. The Wesleyan settlers built a school, followed nine years later by another school. In 1845, the community, with a population of 1143, was an important sealing port, dispatching fifteen vessels to the ice that year. In the early part of this century the population of Cupids had declined to 760. By 1935, the population was down to 562, by 1954 to 476. Incorporation in 1965 brought improved services, facilities and more people and by 1976 the population of Cupids had rebounded to 750.

In 1910, as part of the town's tercentennial celebrations, the Newfoundland Historical Society erected a monument at Cupids in honour of "John Guy, first Governor of Newfoundland, Master of the Bristol Society of Merchant Venturers." The inscription continues: "The plantation which he (Guy) founded in this place then known as Cuper's Cove was the first chartered or lawfully authorized settlement in Newfoundland. In this settlement its founder lived for a season and returned to his native city of Bristol to receive the honours, rewards and esteem of his fellow citizens."

On August 17, 1910 some 3,000 people watched as the second-largest (36 feet by 22 feet) Union Jack in the British Empire was hoisted to the top of a 135-foot tower at Cupids. Governor Sir Ralph Champneys Williams unveiled a plaque at the base of the flagpole to mark the three-hundredth anniversary of the founding of Guy's colony. The huge flag flew proudly until a sleet storm toppled the tower in 1912.

As part of the province's four-hundredth anniversary celebrations in 1983, the Cupids Historical Society and the Newfoundland Historical Society restored the 1910 flagpole. On October 22 of that year the old flag flapped briefly in the breeze before being retired. Then a replica of the original flag ascended the restored tower to serve as a reminder of the colourful history of Newfoundland's valentine town.

PRINCESS PAMELA:
Lady From Fogo

In the spring of 1773 in a drafty, makeshift tilt in a tiny fishing cove on the northeast coast of Newfoundland, a princess was born. This is the true story of the life and times of that little girl who grew up to mingle with the aristocrats of Europe.

In the eighteenth century, this particular corner of North America was subject to attacks by the French and the Americans, who were at odds with the British over fishing, governing and settlement rights. In charge of the four forts and six cannon guarding the small town of Fogo at that time was an English naval officer and merchant by the name of Jeremiah Coughlan.

In the spring of 1771, a lady named Nancy Sims came to work as a domestic servant of Coughlan. It seems that Coughlan took a liking to this young woman and promised to marry her. At the end of the fishing season, as was the custom, Coughlan returned home to England, promising to come back to Newfoundland the following spring. Meanwhile, Nancy, now pregnant with Coughlan's child, went back home to her family's tilt at

Dog Bay, on the island of Newfoundland, for the winter. It was here in this crude little dwelling that Nancy Sims gave birth to her daughter, whom they called Little Nancy.

True to his word, Coughlan came back to Fogo Island that spring and took Nancy and her baby into his comfortable, spacious home at Fogo. He promised to take them back to England that fall where he said he would marry Nancy. However, it wasn't until a year later that the three of them boarded a ship loaded with dried salt fish for the long, exhausting voyage across the Atlantic to Poole, England. In order to simplify matters and avoid unpleasant and unnecessary inquiries, Nancy Sims signed on as the wife of Captain DeBrizey.

We will never know why, but Jeremiah Coughlan never did marry Nancy Sims, who settled at Christchurch, where she earned a meagre living doing expert needlework. On one occasion, she wrote a letter to her brother at Fogo, saying she was too poor to care for her daughter and was moving with her to "foreign parts." In the meantime, Coughlan also wrote to Nancy's brother to say that he knew the whereabouts of the elder Nancy and that Little Nancy was in good hands.

At this point, the elder Nancy fades into the mists of history and we pick up on the story of Little Nancy at the age of six. It so happened that the Duke of Orleans in France was looking for a young, English-speaking girl as a companion for his own daughters who were under the care of Madame de Genlis. The Duke called upon his friend, a Mr. Forth in London, to help him in his search. At Christchurch, Mr. Forth came across young Nancy, a charming, beautiful girl, and persuaded the mother to let her child go across the Channel to France. "I am sending Your Highness the prettiest little girl in England," read

Lady Pamela Fitzgerald and her daughter
Nfld. Book Publishers (1967) Ltd.

part of the letter Forth's valet took back to France along with young Nancy. Madame de Genlis took an instant liking to Nancy, and gave her a new name, Pamela. Eventually, Madame de Genlis contacted Pamela's mother, and paid her twenty-five pounds to relinquish all rights to her own child.

Pamela grew up in regal circles and went to school at Belle Chase, where she rubbed shoulders with princes and princesses. Then, in the late 1780s, the French Revolution rocked the very foundations of one of western Europe's mightiest kingdoms. The Duke of Orleans sent his family, including Pamela, to safety in England, but not before he had commissioned a portrait of the royal household (including Princess Pamela), which still hangs in the palace at Versailles. Of the family's year-long stay in England, famed French author Victor Hugo wrote: "They had only one hundred louis, and lived meanly in furnished apartments." They had two beds, only one with a blanket. At first, Mademoiselle d'Orleans, the Duke's daughter, used the blanket, but one night Madame de Genlis said to her: "You are well and strong; Pamela is cold, so I have put the blanket on her bed."

In England, Pamela and her royal family spent a month at the home of Anglo-Irish dramatist and politician Richard Brinsley Sheridan, then considered the most brilliant man in the whole country. Sheridan courted Pamela and fell in love with her. They became engaged, but for some unknown reason, never became husband and wife.

Not long after, at a performance of the play "Lodoiska", the Irish patriot, Lord Edward Fitzgerald, who had heard of the beautiful Pamela Sims, spied the lady from Fogo sitting in a box next to his. As soon as the curtain fell on the show, Fitzgerald had a friend introduce him to Pamela. Less than a month later, Pamela Sims became Lady Pamela Fitzgerald. The Fitzgeralds returned to London on January 2, 1793; three weeks later they moved into the Kildare homestead at Dublin.

Before long, Lord Fitzgerald, loyal Irishman that he was, became caught up in his country's revolutionary struggle against England. Wherever he went, spies pursued him; the English leaders issued orders for his arrest; he became a fugitive and his life turned into one close call after another. Eventually, three spies caught him in hiding. In the struggle which followed, one of the assailants shot and severely wounded Lord Fitzgerald. He died in agony at his castle a few days later. In his will, he left all to "my wife, Lady Pamela Fitzgerald, as a mark of my esteem, love and confidence in her." Papers seized at Leinster House, the Fitzgerald's residence, suggested that Lady Pamela had been as deeply involved in the Irish revolutionary movement as her husband. As a result, the Privy Council ordered her to leave Ireland. She had given birth to three children for Lord Fitzgerald: a son, Edward; a daughter, Pamela, who married Sir Guy Campbell; and another daughter, Lucy, who married Captain J. F. Lyon.

In 1799, Lady Pamela Fitzgerald went to Hamburg to live with Madame de Genlis. A year later she married Mr. Pitcairn, the U.S. Consul to Germany. Pamela bore a daughter for Pitcairn, but the marriage ended in divorce and Pamela returned to France, adopting the Fitzgerald name once again.

In 1830, the Duke of Orleans, who had once been Pamela's guardian, assumed the throne of France as King Louis Philippe. It seems that the new king and his family pretty well ignored Pamela, who, only a few years earlier, had heard French revolutionaries promise, "She it is whom we will have for our queen."

So, spurned by her former family, a dejected Lady Fitzgerald eventually moved into a French convent, where she died on November 9, 1831 at the age of fifty-five.

In 1847, Reverend Chapman, the S.P.G. missionary at Twillingate, received a letter from Louis Philippe, in which the king inquired about the Sims family of Fogo, making particular mention of Pamela. Reverend Chapman passed the letter on to the Sims family, who, it appears, never did get around to answering it.

In 1880, the descendants of Lady Pamela Fitzgerald moved her ashes from Mont-Martre, France to the family vault at Thames-Ditton, near London. Over the years, the name Sims (which originally may have been spelled Syms) has changed slightly to its present form of Simms. Meanwhile, the intriguing story of the Fogo foundling, whose elegant profile graces a royal portrait in the Palace of Versailles, lives on in the hearts of her descendants and all Newfoundlanders.

GRAND BANK:
Child of the Sea

It's a pretty safe bet that most Canadians have heard of the Grand Banks, the famous fishing grounds which cover some 36,000 square miles south of the island of Newfoundland. There's also a town called Grand Bank, which nudges its nautical namesake.

Grand Bank was born of the sea and is still a child of the sea, cradled in a small cove on the toe of the fog-shrouded Burin Peninsula. This town, like many Newfoundland communities, has always depended on the providence of the intemperate ocean for its very existence. Grand Bank is the quintessential Newfoundland fishing community, its small harbour offering welcome protection from the choppy waters of Fortune Bay, its old fishermen's houses with their "widow's walks" looking out on the ocean, its historic business premises of wood and stone standing as monuments to another era, its inhabitants redolent with the salty, storied, often tragic essence of a seafaring heritage.

Historians believe Grand Bank started out as a French fishing settlement around 1640. A French census of

1687 put the population of "Grand Banc" at forty-five: thirty-nine servants, two masters, three women and one child. The report also noted that the community had three houses, one church and eighteen muskets. Later French censuses – in 1691, 1693 and 1694 – included information on the settlement of "Grand Banc." Some time after that, the British took control of the area. From the records of British fishing admirals we learn that, in 1740, Grand Bank had seven masters, forty-seven manservants, three mistresses and seven children.

After the 1763 Treaty of Paris gave Britain the northern part of North America, except for St. Pierre and Miquelon, many English-speaking people moved from St. Pierre to the Burin Peninsula, including Grand Bank. Even today, most of the surnames of Grand Bank – Stoodley, Patten, Forsey, Buffett, Douglas, Follett – are of obvious English origin. A census taken in 1827-28 put the population of Grand Bank at 261, mostly Protestants. These days, Grand Bank is home to around 4,000 people.

Sea disasters are nothing new to most Newfoundland fishing communities. The very name Grand Bank calls to mind such disasters as the sinking of the schooner Russell Lake, with Captain Frank Stoodley and his crew of four on March 17, 1929, the loss of the banking schooner Partanna with its twenty-five men in April, 1936, the loss of the Blue Wave with all hands on February 10, 1959, the sinking of the Blue Mist II with her thirteen-man crew in February, 1966.

A few sea stories associated with Grand Bank have happier endings – like the time a British ship rescued the crew of the schooner Max Horton on March 28, 1926, or when rescuers saved the crew of the Flower Dew, 200 miles off Savannah, Georgia on October 15, 1927, or when the crew of the Marion Mosher rowed ashore after their schooner burned off St. Pierre on December 23, 1948. The list of ocean dramas that have touched the people of this community goes on and on.

The attractive Grand Bank Fishermen's Museum, which Premier Joey Smallwood had the foresight to salvage from Expo 67 (the museum was part of the Yugoslavian Pavilion at Expo), serves as a repository of the maritime history of the south coast.

Like many Newfoundland communities, Grand Bank has turned out a generous number of prominent citizens. Dozens of sea captains, for example, with names like Stoodley, Walters, Snook, Thornhill, Moulton and Rose came from this seafaring town. A glimpse at some others reads like a veritable *Who's Who?* Roland

Port of Grand Bank Nfld. Dept. of Development

Thornhill served as a cabinet minister in the Nova Scotia government; lawyer T. Alex Hickman served as Newfoundland's Chief Justice; Newfoundland Prime Minister Albert E. Hickman came from Grand Bank; the late Dr. Eugene Forsey was a senator in Ottawa; the Hon. Philip Samuel Forsey served in an earlier Newfoundland government. The list would be incomplete without mention of former Mayor Fred Tessier who, in recognition of his tireless efforts on behalf of the municipality, earned the unofficial title "Mr. Grand Bank."

The economy of Grand Bank reached its peak during the latter part of the last century, when the great two and three-masted banking schooners fished the rich waters along the south coast. As an elderly Grand Bank merchant told writer Harold Horwood some years ago: "We didn't always have this Sunday morning look, not when we had nineteen bankers sailing out of this harbour. Why, we had a beach – just our own firm – where you could spread 2,500 quintals of fish.... All the Bank fish was made by women – every cod's tail – and a hundred women might share a thousand dollars between them.... But, it's over now, of course. Today, you've got to stand in line in Grand Bank to buy a salt fish when a bit of it arrives at the store."

Just as elsewhere in Newfoundland, the church figures prominently in the life of Grand Bank, with Salvation Army families making up the largest congregation. "The Army" has been a visible part of Grand Bank life since the late 1800s.

The community is looking after its senior citizens too. The town's Interfaith Home for the elderly is home for seniors from all along the south coast.

John Burke High School, my alma mater of which I have many pleasant memories, burned down some years ago. Today, a new modern building of the same name stands in its place. The school is named for Dr. John Burke, who graduated from Dalhousie University in 1919 and served as medical doctor for the area for forty-one years. In 1948, Dr. Burke was designated a Companion of the British Empire by King George VI. In the early 1970s, funding from the federal government financed the building of a modern elementary school, Partanna Academy.

I have many fond memories too of the overwhelming friendliness of the people of Grand Bank, a friendliness I can assure you is unsurpassed anywhere in a province noted for its hospitality. Even the omnipresent fog which rolls in over the Burin Peninsula does nothing to dampen the affability of these fine, gentle people.

One sure way to get sports fans on the Burin Peninsula excited is to mention soccer, the "official" sport of this part of the province. The Grand Bank GeeBees have long been one of the top teams on the Peninsula. There has always been a strong rivalry between Grand Bank and Fortune in many respects, but the competition is particularly intense when the outcome of a soccer match is at stake. Anyway you look at it, Grand Bank is certainly up to giving the visitor a taste of the real Newfoundland.

NEWFOUNDLAND'S PUGILISTS:
Punching It Out

When most people think of boxing in the Atlantic Provinces, they might tend to think of Nova Scotia and its longstanding tradition of turning out scrappers like Clyde Gray, Chris Clarke, Ray Downey and Wayne Gordon. But its fair to say that Newfoundland, too, has produced a good share of tough punchers. While I'm not one to get all fired up about a boxing match, unless we're talking about the likes of an Ali-Frazier matchup, I will concede that history is history, whether inside or outside the boxing ropes.

A number of notable characters have danced and jabbed their way through boxing circles in this province over the years. Some well-known examples come to mind – Johnny Dwyer, Mike Shallow, Arthur Johnson, Bill Drover, Terry Hayward.

Born in St. John's in 1845, John J. Dwyer moved to Brooklyn, New York, where he worked as an apprentice printer before taking up boxing professionally. On May 8, 1879, Dwyer captured both the American and World heavyweight boxing titles in a thirteen-minute bare-knuckle fight against James Elliott at Long Point, Ontario. Ironically, bare-knuckle fighting was illegal on the American side of the border. "His limbs are thoroughly hardened and his hands are solid as iron," wrote a Brooklyn Eagle reporter describing Dwyer.

Another Newfoundland boxer, Mike Shallow, was born in 1874 at Fermeuse on the southern shore of the Avalon Peninsula. Shallow also moved to the States – to Boston – at a young age and took up boxing there. Returning to his native sod in the early 1900s, Shallow became even more heavily involved in boxing. His reputation grew, until fights in England in 1904 and 1905 brought him the heavyweight crown of the British

Postcard of Hopson vs Blackmore Fight, Grand Falls July 30, 1923
Ron Ennis, The Advertiser

Empire.

Shallow then moved to the central Newfoundland town of Grand Falls, where he started his own boxing club and did much to promote the sport in the central part of the island. Probably Shallow's most celebrated match in Newfoundland took place at the Prince's Rink in St. John's, where he battled Jack Monroe of Montana to a draw. Monroe himself earned a measure of distinction, after he won a decision over Jim Jeffries, who became world boxing champion in 1899. On April 24, 1976, the Newfoundland Sports Hall of Fame inducted Mike Shallow into its select ranks.

Another fighter well known in the central Newfoundland region was Bill Howse, who boxed at Shallow's club in Grand Falls. Of the fourteen fights he sparred in between 1936 and 1941, Howse won twelve, tied one and lost only one. On April 18, 1940, he won the Newfoundland amateur lightweight title by a knockout over Bill Whyte of St. John's.

The 1920s were a great time for amateur boxing in Newfoundland, with the colony producing fighters like Frank Stamp, Sam LaFosse, Harold Diamond and Mike O'Brien. LaFosse, a southpaw with a "deadly punch", held the Newfoundland bantamweight title for ten years and represented Newfoundland at the British Empire Games in Hamilton, Ontario in 1930. Although never officially confirmed, reports indicated that LaFosse tied for the bronze medal at those games, in spite of a severe attack of arthritis. LaFosse never did receive a medal for that achievement, but his name appears in the Guinness Book of British Empire and Commonwealth Games Records.

Arthur Johnson established his boxing reputation at McGill University, where he won the bantamweight championship in 1921. He then went on to win the Canadian intercollegiate final. The Newfoundland Sports Hall of Fame made Johnson a member on October 15, 1977. Two other boxers, Hepburn Elliott of St. John's and Cecil Brain of Grand Falls achieved much the same measure of distinction as Arthur Johnson.

While amateur boxing had been growing briskly in Newfoundland, professional boxing didn't really get official sanction until the fall of 1930, although the occasional bout had been staged before that. In the late 1930s, the professional side of the sport one again fell off. Not until the 1950s, with the appearance of characters like Bernie "Boom Boom" Skanes, Joe "Brick" Wall and Phonse LeSage (who fought a match with Yvon Durelle), did professional boxing stage a comeback in Newfoundland. The main problem was simply the shortage of professional fighters. Since amateurs and professionals were not permitted to fight on the same card, promoters would get around this restriction by putting on amateur fights, taking a fifteen-minute break, then staging professional bouts.

Another Newfoundland fighter worth mentioning is Scottish-born Bill Drover, who grew up at Hodge's Cove, Trinity Bay. In the early 1960s, Drover, while still an amateur, won the Central Army Eastern Ontario, Canadian Army Central Command, and Canadian Army heavyweight titles. Drover then turned professional and took the Eastern Canada heavyweight title from Earl Pilgrim. Drover later went to live in Montreal and fought in England and South Africa. At one point in the 1970s he was a serious contender for the Canadian heavyweight title then held by George Chuvalo. His scheduled bid to take Chuvalo's crown was halted after Drover twisted his back while training. Drover lost a fight to

British Empire and European heavyweight champion Joe Bugner in London, England.

Junior middleweight Terry Hayward from Port au Port on the west coast also made a name for himself in boxing circles, winning the Eastern Canada title in 1970. Later, in Labrador City, Hayward defeated Montrealer Dave Hilton in a match Hayward believed would give him the Canadian title, but the Canadian Boxing Federation refused to acknowledge the win because the match had not been held at a recognized centre.

Amateur boxer Derek Hancock, who played for the St. John's Capitals hockey team, captured the Newfoundland Golden Gloves Award in 1970 and went on to compete in the Eastern Canada championship in Montreal. In 1979, Hancock was elected to the Newfoundland House of Assembly. It's been a while, but perhaps one of those years, Newfoundlanders may once again punch their way onto the world boxing map.

SIGNAL HILL:
Sentinel of History

A motel perched on the western flank of Signal Hill calls itself "The Inn With The View." Well, Signal Hill itself could rightly be called "The Hill With The View" - a sweeping view of the old port city, the Narrows, Pleasantville (former site of an American military base), the historic little village of Quidi Vidi, and the limitless expanse of the Atlantic stretching away to the east. At its highest point, Signal Hill might even qualify as a small mountain, rising to more than 500 feet.

The name of this famous natural landmark which guards the entrance to St. John's dates back to the end of the sixteenth century. At that time, British settlers put up fortifications at several locations near the entrance to St. John's and Quidi Vidi and put cannons in place to signal the approach of ships. The ships which came by weren't always friendly, and more than a few skirmishes developed between these visitors and the local residents or soldiers. The practice of firing off the noon-day gun atop Signal Hill dates back to the early 1800s.

Cabot Tower, duplicate of another tower of the same

name at Bristol, England, was built in the late 1890s to commemorate John Cabot's voyage to Newfoundland four hundred years earlier. The opening of the tower also coincided with Queen Victoria's Diamond Jubilee. On December 12, 1901, in an old hospital building on Signal Hill, with the wind roaring outside, Italian Guglielmo Marconi, flying a kite high over the hill for better reception on his wireless, deciphered the three dots of the letter "S", being transmitted from Poldhu, Cornwall, on the other side of the Atlantic. A plaque near Cabot Tower marks this milestone in international communication.

Until 1958, flags and pennants flapped regularly atop the tower to announce the arrival of ships to the port of St. John's. In 1958, the Canadian government declared Signal Hill a National Historic Site. Certainly, none of the many such sites across the country is more deserving of this designation, as a look at just some of its rich history proves.

Unfortunately for the earliest British settlers, the hill did not always stand up under attack, because it had not been fortified. In the winter of 1696-97, the Frenchman d'Iberville and his forces captured St. John's and most of the Avalon Peninsula. Before long, the British took the territory back, then constructed Fort William and Fort George near the entrance to St. John's harbour. Again, in 1708, the French, this time under the command of Sieur de St. Ovide, took St. John's and demolished its fortifications. But building a fort near the top of Signal Hill was still not considered practicable.

In 1756, England and France began their Seven Years War. By the end of the War, France had lost control of many of its North American holdings; in 1762, a fleet of ships set out from Brest, France, with the aim of wresting back control of Newfoundland from British hands. In June of that year, fifteen hundred men led by Comte d'Haussonville, along with four ships under the command of Captain Temay, stormed St. John's and seized the town. The French captors decided to repair the ruined forts of St. John's and to build a new fortification on Signal Hill.

It goes without saying that the British were not content to abandon the vital port of St. John's, at least not without putting up a solid struggle. With a fleet of ships commanded by Lord Colville and an infantry force led by Lieutenant-Colonel William Amherst, in whose honour Fort Amherst was named, the British landed at Torbay, just a few miles north of St. John's and pushed

Cabot Tower Calvin Coish

toward Signal Hill. By daybreak on September 12, the British had taken control of the old hill and turned the cannons towards French fortifications near the harbour entrance. Six days later, d'Haussonville dispatched a letter of surrender to William Amherst. Upon surrendering, d'Haussonville requested that his troops be permitted to keep their personal goods and essential supplies. It's been reported that Amherst, taking offence to the request, replied that "His Britannic Majesty's troops never pillage."

The 1762 Battle of Signal Hill was reportedly the last military clash between British and French forces in North America. A few years later, during the Napoleonic Wars, a French fleet approached St. John's, but turned and sailed away after sizing up the city's impressive defences. The fleet then moved on to pillage Petty Harbour and Bay Bulls.

William Amherst realized that St. John's was an ideal site from which to fend off attacks. The area was, he reported, "the most advantageous ground I ever saw ... really almost incredible." Towards the end of the eighteenth century, the British further reinforced the defences around St. John's, putting up more batteries, barracks, hot-shot furnaces, a blockhouse, storehouse, powder magazine, even a concrete wall on Signal Hill. The vast maze of defensive installations earned the hill the nickname, "Fort Impregnable." Nevertheless, the Royal Engineers kept pushing for additional fortifications. In 1809, Lieutenant-Colonel E. E. Durnford drew up plans for a huge defence citadel that would cover the top of Signal Hill, but these plans were never carried out.

After the Napoleonic Wars, Britian relaxed its defence of Newfoundland and the fortifications on Signal Hill gradually fell into disrepair. By the middle of the nineteenth century, the hill was being used only as a spot to signal the approach of ships. In fact, a signal mast and crossarm still stand on the roof of Cabot Tower.

In 1696, the British built Crow's Nest Battery on Gibbett Hill. The name of that hill comes from the fact that a gibbett was constructed there in 1750 for the execution of criminals. Standing atop Gibbett Hill, one gets an eerie feeling of witnessing scenes from one of Signal Hill's more gruesome chapters.

Today, Queen's Battery, near the top of Signal Hill, consists of half a dozen cannons fronting the remnants of stone barracks, powder magazines and other structures built in the late 1700s. The cannons, now fixed firmly in place for safety's sake, could once be rotated on tracks to

Queen's Battery Calvin Coish

SIGNAL HILL

take aim at the Narrows, St. John's harbour, and points in between. Looking down from Queen's Battery, you can see Chain Rock, to which a chain and log boom, strung across the Narrows, were attached in order to keep enemy ships and submarines from entering the almost landlocked harbour. History tells us that in the 1670s a gun battery on Chain Rock blasted warnings to Dutch pirates outside the harbour.

They say Ladies Lookout on Signal Hill got its name in the early 1700s, since it was a convenient spot from which ladies could watch for approaching ships carrying enemy forces or returning husbands, brothers and fathers. Rising to a height of 525 feet, Ladies Lookout offers its own splendid view for 360 degrees. Nearby are the uncovered remnants of a canteen, an ale storage hut, a latrine and an ash pit used by British soldiers.

The Signal Hill Tattoo has been a big attraction ever since 1967, when the spectacle began as an Opportunities for Youth project. The Tattoo presents marching soldiers and mock battles, complete with clattering rifles and booming cannons echoing out over the Narrows. The colourful pageantry of this summertime exhibition can be considered the equivalent of the Changing of the Guard or the Mounties' Musical Ride.

Just in the shadow of the hilltop, there's an interpretation and visitor's centre – an attractive, low, stone building containing audio-visual displays which depict the history of Signal Hill and Newfoundland. From the Centre, you can take a stroll along trails leading to Gibbett Hill, Queen's Battery, Cabot Tower and Ladies' Lookout. If you wish, your car can take you close to Cabot Tower or Queen's Battery.

The feeling of standing where hundreds of British and

DISTANT SHORES

French soldiers lived, fought and died for centuries, and the unrivalled view of St. John's and the vast Atlantic draw hundreds of thousands of visitors to Signal Hill every year. Slowly, the grand old bastion is beginning to give us a glimpse of its history, but there's still a lot of this rich past left to discover.

Signal Hill Tattoo Calvin Coish

FISHING ON THE LABRADOR:
Good Times And Bad

Before the eighteenth century, European fishermen showed little interest in the rugged, sparsely-populated chunk of rocky territory known as Labrador, even though the waters offshore swarmed with codfish. But, after 1713, the French set up temporary fishing communities on the southern coast of Labrador. Fifty years later, after the British conquest of Quebec, English merchants rushed to cash in on the cod, seal and salmon fisheries in this corner of North America.

Still, not many people rushed to settle on these desolate shores. The short Labrador fishing season made it unprofitable to own a schooner to be used solely for fishing there. After 1795, that situation changed, because the same vessels could take part in the spring seal hunt and the summer fishery in Labrador.

Each year, in the early part of March, hundreds of men would travel to St. John's to get a berth on one of the sealing ships. Then, in late April or early May, the seal hunt over, many of those same men would start to get ready for the Labrador summer fishery. Come late

DISTANT SHORES

Collector boat leaving Fishing Ship's Harbour

Decks Awash

May or early June, the ships would head northward from ports along the east coast of Newfoundland; a week or ten days later they would reach their destination in Labrador.

Traditionally, two groups from the island of Newfoundland got in on the annual Labrador fishery. One group, called floaters, sailed north in schooners, which served as their base of operations for the summer. In his book, *The Letter That Was Never Read: A History of the Labrador Fishery*, Benjamin J. Powell, Sr. painted this picture in words: "It was a handsome sight to watch these vessels sail north in June. Often they would reach for miles with their rails washing the water, the sun sparkling in the rigging and most of them carrying a big fishing boat in tow on a long rope."

The other group of fishermen, called stationers, most of them from Conception Bay, set up summer living quarters in various coves and inlets along the Labrador coast. The stationers often travelled to Labrador as passengers on the floaters' schooners.

In 1820, a Captain Robinson, who had been sent to Labrador to settle a legal wrangle, reported that, "In all harbours where there are any considerable fisheries, a few people winter to take care of the property, cut wood, and catch furs. These constitute the only resident population." It was estimated that each small Labrador community produced "about 1,500 quintals on an average, making about 20,000 (in total); with a proportion of oil, at the rate of one ton for every 200 quintals of fish. At all the small intermediate harbours, there is an appearance of settling and building houses, but we cannot estimate their produce at all correctly; though, from the number of Newfoundland and Nova Scotia vessels which carry on a desultory fishing and take away their cargoes, a very considerable quantity of fish may be added to the above estimate, perhaps 20,000 quintals."

Until around 1870, the stationers caught their fish mainly by hook and line, while the schooners used cod nets and seines. Records show that, during the 1870s, thousands of people in hundreds of boats took part in the Labrador fishery. By 1890, cod traps had become popular with both stationers and floater schooners. But, when fish were scarce, they turned to the hook and line again. Floater fishermen had an advantage over the stationers in that they could move around until they found the best fishing spots. In 1890, 10,450 men, 2,065 women, 828 children and 861 schooners were involved in the fishery in Labrador. Before long, however, the fortunes of the Labrador fishery took a turn downward. The short fishing season and uncertain weather made it hard to produce fish of a high quality and prices dropped, depressed even further by growing competition from France and the Scandinavian countries.

Schooner fishing generally started in the Strait of Belle Isle just after the middle of July and gradually edged northward along the Labrador coast. In a good season, a schooner might make two bumper trips.

So, for years, fishermen and their families from the island of Newfoundland would head off to places like Batteau, Indian Tickle, Murray's Harbour, Spotted Islands, Black Tickle and Packs Harbour, sometimes setting up living quarters practically next door to full-time residents of Labrador, nicknamed livyers, because, as they said, "we lives yer." Some years, as many as 20,000 men, women and children (out of the island's population of some 150,000) took part in this annual trek northward. In fact, without the dollars generated by the Labrador fishery, the economy of Newfoundland would have been much more anemic.

Conditions in Labrador, especially for the stationers in their ramshackle huts, were often far from pleasant. In his history of Labrador, W. G. Gosling wrote: "It had long been known that vessels going to Labrador were systematically overcrowded with passengers - men, women and children. The Labrador planters took with them not only their servants for the fishery, male and female, but also their whole families, their goats, their pigs, their dogs and their fowls. Seventy to eighty persons were often crowded into a little schooner of about forty tons. There were no conveniences of any kind, and no separation of the sexes. Decency was impossible and vice was flagrant."

No longer willing to ignore reports of the "scandalous condition of things," the Newfoundland Government appointed a Commission of Inquiry and, in 1881, passed an act requiring separate quarters for females and limiting the number of passengers each vessel could carry.

By the 1920s, the Labrador fishery came under heavy pressure, as Italy, Spain and Portugal sent out their own subsidized fleets of fishing vessels. The demand for salt fish from Labrador declined while the demand for fresh fish increased. Because of the short drying season, most Labrador fish had to be "heavy salted", in order to preserve it. Unless the fish was carefully processed and handled properly it tended to develop a bacterial growth called "pink", in warm climates where it was sold.

In the 1930s, a drastic failure of the cod fishery in Conception Bay sent many fishermen back to the Labrador. The hours were long, the work backbreaking, and the pay was by no means excessive - a mere fifty or sixty dollars a man during a good summer, less than that some years.

Little wonder then that the Second World War drew many able-bodied men away from the fishery. On one of the American bases set up in Newfoundland, a person could earn forty to fifty cents an hour. It isn't surprising then that many men had no great desire to go back to earning three dollars for each quintal of fish caught and cured, with no guarantee they would take home even a cent.

After World War II, fishermen on the island of Newfoundland began marketing their own fish, which was thicker and had a higher fat content than fish caught off Labrador; this Newfoundland fish was even more susceptible than Labrador fish to the dreaded pink. It became more and more difficult to sell fish from any part of Newfoundland, including Labrador. In the 1950s, after repeated pleas to the federal government for assistance fell on deaf ears, the Labrador fishery declined even further, but managed to survive. Eventually, collector boats began calling in at the harbours and coves in Labrador to pick up the perishable catches of fish and deliver them to refrigerated facilities.

In 1986, the people of Carbonear held their first Stationers Festival, to celebrate their long history of making the voyage north to the rich fishing grounds off the mainland part of Newfoundland. These days, instead of heading off to Labrador to catch fish, most people along the east coast of Newfoundland just rely on their memories of this chapter in our maritime history.

GREENSPOND:
Outport Legacy

In many ways it's not much different from dozens of other villages dotting the Newfoundland coastline. It still relies on an increasingly precarious fishery for its existence. In Newfoundland terms, it went from big town to small town. Early settlers cut down most of its cover of coniferous trees. It's a small, rocky island on the northern side of Bonavista Bay and its name is Greenspond. Some years ago it got a causeway link with the main island of Newfoundland.

Where did the name Greenpsond come from? Some contend the name originated with the harbour, a small saltwater pond which was at one time surrounded by lots of trees. Another plausible explanation for the name is that it came from a combination of two of the community's earliest surnames - Green and Pond.

In its heyday, Greenspond's prominence as a fishing, shipping and general commercial centre earned it the nickname "Capital of the North". In 1703, the community harvested 1,800 quintals of cod; in 1706, it produced 100 quintals of salmon. By the early 1700s,

Greenspond had established a flourishing trade with Portugal, a trade it later extended to other countries. Records for the period from 1838 to 1850 show that ships set out from Greenspond bound for Britain, Portugal, Spain, Italy, Brazil, Greece and Ireland. Most of these ships carried dried codfish and returned with salt, which, of course, would be used for curing more codfish. Some ships which sailed from Greenspond also carried blubber and oil, dried caplin, furs, barrel staves, pickled salmon, whalebone and berries and brought back various drygoods, wine and fruit. In 1854, the community of Greenspond chalked up quite a favourable balance of payments when it exported products worth close to 24,000 pounds and imported goods worth less than 9,000 pounds.

Records show that the first people settled at Greenspond in the late seventeenth century. In 1713, under the Treaty of Utrecht, Greenspond became part of the French Shore, a stretch of Newfoundland coastline open to French fishing vessels. Declining fish catches between 1713 and 1728 led to a decline in the population of Greenspond. Then, in the 1730s, the codfish came back to the waters near this tiny island, and more settlers, including some Irish immigrants, made Greenspond their home. The influx of new people continued until the 1740s, when fish catches again fell off.

For twenty years the fish stayed away, and the fishermen of Greenspond sailed farther afield in search of cod. As a result, many Greenspond fishermen took to sailing their vessels north every summer to the rich fishing grounds along the Labrador coast.

By the latter part of the eighteenth century, Greenspond had a more or less stable population of around 300 people. In 1807, the 215 fishermen and sixty shoremen at Greenspond landed and cured some 11,000 quintals of fish, produced 130 tons of oil and harvested 17,000 seal pelts.

The town had a visiting Anglican minister and, in 1784, gained the services of a magistrate. In 1796, Wesleyan Methodism came to Greenspond when Reverend George Smith, an itinerant missionary stationed at Trinity, organized a small Methodist "class". Reverend John Corlett revived Smith's efforts in July of 1826, but it was not until 1862 that the town got its first resident Methodist minister, Reverend John Allen.

Greenspond got its first church (St. Stephen's Church of England) in 1812, thanks largely to Governor Duckworth, who had visited the community two years earlier. It was not until 1829 that the town got its first resident clergyman, Rev. N. A. Coster. In 1849, Rev. Julian Moreton wrote that "the mission of Greenspond (is) the largest ... in the diocese of Newfoundland, extending along seventy miles of coast and requiring a journey of 200 miles to visit all its stations."

The Church's influence notwithstanding, social conditions at Greenspond weren't always as refined as they could have been. A Wesleyan minister who visited Greenspond in 1866 reported that there were five "public houses" there and he called the town the "Sodom of the North." Another clergyman at the time wrote that "moral conditions left much to be desired ... drinking, swearing and adultery were rife; Sunday in the summer season was a market day." In the late 1800s, the Salvation Army came to Greenspond, attracting so many converts that they built their own citadel. Over the years since then, many prominent people have come from the Salvation Army Corps at Greenspond, including

Brigadier Walter Oakley, who became principal of the Salvation Army Training College at St. John's.

With the churches came schools and education. In 1815, residents of Grenspond appealed to the governor to appoint Thomas Walley as layreader since he was "capable of teaching the children to read, write and cypher, etc." The SPG (Society for the Propagation of the Gospel) did in fact appoint Walley as layreader, and, by 1828, Greenspond had 186 day school, 200 Sunday School, and seventy-five adult school students. In September, 1850, the teacher and layreader, Mr. Dyer, wrote in his journal that a visiting judge had said that the school at Greenspond was "the largest in the island, larger than St. John's." Over the years since then, the schools of Greenspond have turned out many fine people – like politician, businessman and poet A. C. Wornell, politician Walter Carter, lawyer and politician Sydney Dara Blandford, and deaconesses Annie Wornell and Stella Burry.

The Roman Catholic population at Greenspond was always a small minority. In 1826, the town was home to 500 Protestants and 100 Catholics. In 1874, the town's 1,445 Protestants vastly outnumbered the seventy-nine Roman Catholics living there. In 1901, there were only eighteen Roman Catholics among the total population of 1,726.

By the middle of the nineteenth century, the seal hunt was a central part of the economy of Greenspond, and the community had developed into a major supply centre and clearing port for ships sailing to Labrador to catch cod or to the ice floes to hunt seals. In 1860, eighteen ships carrying crews of fifteen to twenty men each took part in the annual spring seal harvest out of Greenspond. Thirty-five years later, the number of sealing ships setting out from this port had fallen to nine, but the ships were now bigger and stronger and carried an average crew of around 210 men.

Eventually, the merchants of St. John's took over the commercial side of the sealing industry, but Greenspond continued to be a departure point for ships bound for Labrador, until the Labrador fishery itself slid into decline during World War II.

This little chunk of Newfoundland granite has produced a good share of famous sealing captains. Like Captain Darius Blandford, who, in 1901, as captain of the Southern Cross, made "the quickest trip ever recorded", returning to port with a full load of seal pelts in just under eleven days. In 1884, Captain Samuel Blandford, brother of Darius, in the SS Neptune, brought in the largest number of seals ever landed by a wooden steamer - 42,242. Four days later, he set a weight record for wooden walls when he landed more than 884 tons of sealskins. Then there were the Carters - Alexander (Sandy), Augustus (Gus) and Peter - the latter bringing ashore 49,259 seals weighing a record 1,256 tons, in 1933, on board the SS Ungava.

The people of Greenspond have witnessed numerous shipping disasters and have given shelter to more than a few unfortunate sailors. In fact, at times, shipwrecks turned out to be a rather sizable source of extra income for some residents of the town. In February, 1867, for instance, William Yetman of Greenspond recived compensation for "dieting" thirty-five men from the sealing ship Amazon for four days and for providing four coffins. A year later, "142 men and women and eighteen children" from the wreck Adamant were housed and fed at Greenspond. In June of 1870, records show that "Dr. Skelton attended the sick at a cost of two pounds" and

"George Bridle boarded ten men" from the Othello.

One businessman who opened a store at Greenspond in the 1860s was a former Prince Edward Islander named David Smallwood, grandfather of Newfoundland's first premier, Joey Smallwood. The construction of a bait depot at Greenspond in 1946 helped in part to compensate for the drop in the Labrador fishery, but the depot closed about twenty years later. A fresh fish processing plant employing fifty persons opened in 1957, but it closed ten years later. In the mid-1970s, a smokehouse opened in the building which had been the bait depot, providing a market for catches of salmon and codfish. The smokehouse is no longer operating, nor is the town's fish plant, shut down by the devastating moratorium on codfishing.

At the turn of the century, Greenspond was home to more than 1,700 people. These days, between four and five hundred make their home on this little island. Some residents have been pushing to have Greenspond declared a heritage village. A fitting designation that would be, for here you will find the quintessential Newfoundland outport, complete with its old fishermen's houses, unique dialect, culture and customs, its seaweed-covered rocks washed by the relentless, restless sea.

TREPASSEY:
River of Roses

On September 18, 1986, two vintage Second World War Catalina flying boats made a special landing at Trepassey, a small community of around 1,500 people tucked into a cozy indraft on the southern shore of the Avalon Peninsula. The landing marked the fiftieth anniversary of the first trans-Atlantic crossing by United States naval aircraft, which used the long, sheltered, ice-free harbour at Trepassey as a base on this side of the Atlantic.

In 1927, Italian aviator Colonel Francisco de Pinedo landed at Trepassey, after circumnavigating the South Atlantic in the Santa Maria II. The next year, William Stultz, Lou Gordon and Amelia Earhart lifted off the water at Trepassey in the hydroplane Friendship, bound for Southampton, England, and Earhart flew into the history books as the first woman to cross the Atlantic by air.

The Portuguese called this place by the lyrical name Rio de Rosas (River of Roses). The present name comes from the French trepasser, meaning to die, and it is indeed true that many a sailor or fisherman lost his life in the treacherous waters which lash this rugged coast.

In the early sixteenth century, Trepassey was an important fishing station for fishermen from Europe. In 1616, Welsh nobleman Sir William Vaughan, who apparently never did set foot on Newfoundland soil, bought a tract of land on the Avalon Peninsula from the London and Bristol Company, with the idea of turning the area into a new Cambriol or Wales. At Trepassey, Vaughan planned to set up his capital, which was to be named Cambriol Colchos. Records suggest that Trepassey was first settled between 1617 and 1622.

In 1620, Governor Richard Whitbourne compared Trepassey to the town of Trinity, on the Bonavista

Trepassey Nfld. Dept. of Development

Peninsula. "Trepassey in like manner is as commodious a harbour," Whitbourne wrote, "and is both faire and pleasant, and (has) a wholesome coast free from rock and shelves (shoals), so that ... it lies the south-most of any harbour in the land, and most conveniently to receive our shipping passing to and from Virginia, and the Bermuda Islands; and also any other shipping that shall passe to and from the River of Canady (the St. Lawrence) and the coast thereof; because they usually passe, and so return in sight of the land of Trepassey."

In spite of Trepassey's commanding position relative to the shipping lanes, it seems that the colony struggled to survive. The land eventually passed to Lord Falkland and Lord Baltimore, neither of whom managed to turn Trepassey into a major shipping port.

In 1628, Lord Baltimore, Governor at Ferryland, forty miles north of Trepassey, launched a retaliatory attack against the French who occupied Trepassey. Using only two ships, the Victory and the Benediction, Baltimore took the French by surprise and captured six of their fishing ships.

Some years later, in the 1670s, we find George and Richard Periman from North Devonshire living at Trepassey, where they managed up to a dozen fishing boats and employed as many as sixty men. In 1681, Trepassey had a small, year-round population of forty-one people and a summer population of 200, with English and French getting along peacefully side by side.

Under the Treaty of Utrecht in 1713, England gained full control of Trepassey and English merchants from Topsham moved to the colony. Some of the earliest settlers were the Follettes and the Jacksons. They were followed by people with surnames like Devereaux, Curtis, Sutton, Waddleton, Corrigan and O'Brien.

In 1730, pirate Bartholomew Roberts raided the harbour of Trepassey, sinking all but one of the twenty-two ships there and destroying the plantations. Local legend holds that, before he headed to the comfort of tropical climes, Roberts buried some of his loot at a place called Quarry's Rock, near Northwest River. As far as we can tell, no one has yet found that treasure.

Following the American Revolution of 1776, the Grand Banks fishery to the south of Trepassey went into decline. Although there were 129 vessels fishing out of this area in 1787, depressed markets for fish took their toll on the economy.

During the 1800s, fishermen in the Trepassey area were using two kinds of vessels. Some fished with jiggers, nets or trawls from two-man dories, landing anywhere from four to fifteen quintals of fish per trip. Others fished from larger skiffs, with up to seven crewmen using jiggers, nets, trawls or cod seines. Each of these larger boats could carry more than 30 quintals of fish.

In 1836, 247 people lived at Trepassey. By 1851, the figure was up to 541. In 1901, there were 793 people living here; by 1971, the population had rebounded to 1,027.

During the depression that hit Newfoundland after the First World War, many people from Trepassey and other parts of Newfoundland headed off to greener pastures in Boston, New York and other cities along the eastern seabord of the United States. Until recently, the main source of employment at Trepassey was the fish plant, which opened in the early 1950s. Recently, there has been talk of Chinese interests making use of the idle premises.

This area of the province has always been predominantly Roman Catholic. In 1779, for example, there were 192 settlers of Irish descent and sixty-eight of English descent at Trepassey. In 1804, the number of Irish residents stood at 221, while only six were of English stock. It is not surprising, then, that the Presentation Sisters have been part of life at Trepassey ever since Bishop Thomas Power opened a convent here in 1882.

The local Nurse Abernethy Clinic gets its name from a nurse who came to the south coast of Newfoundland in 1939. Christina (Smith) Abernethy set up a nursing station at Trepassey in the early 1950s and stayed there until she retired in 1965. The Royal Canadian Legion named Nurse Abernethy its Woman of the Year in 1976. "Never Her Equal Again!" declared a headline in the *Daily News* of June 16, 1978.

If you're a tourist, you'll be pleased to know there's a travel trailer park between Northwest River and Biscay Bay River, two popular salmon rivers not far from Trepassey. Nearby, you might be lucky enough to catch sight of some members of the local herd of 3,000 caribou. Like many other Newfoundland communities, Trepassey celebrates its own civic holiday, Trepassey Day. Judging from its rich history and civic pride, this place has quite a lot to celebrate.

NEWFOUNDLAND SHIPWRECKS:
The Way Of The Sea

Shipwrecks have been a fact of life (and death) as long as men have sailed the seven seas. No one knows for certain exactly how many ships have come to grief along the rocky, stormwsept coastline of Newfoundland.

Sometime around the year 1500, Italian explorer John Cabot reportedly lost a ship on his second voyage to these parts. In the late 1500s, several Basque whaling ships - like the San Juan, discovered by Selma Barkham at Red Bay, Labrador some years ago - surrendered to assault by savage seas. In 1696, at Bay Bulls, near St. John's, a British frigate, the Sapphire (referred to in French records as the Zephyr), went to the bottom after a battle with French ships Philippeaux and Comte de Toulouse. As with many shipwrecks, details concerning the occasion are scanty, obscured by close to 300 years of myth and mystery.

Countless ships have met their doom all along the rugged shoreline of Newfoundland, but the southern end of the Avalon Peninsula can make a legitimate claim to the title "Graveyard of the Atlantic." Some years ago, professor Thomas F. Nemec of Memorial University documented more than 300 shipwrecks which occurred along that stretch of steep cliffs and treacherous shoals. During the forty years up to 1904, 2,000 people lost their lives in a total of ninety-four shipwrecks near Cape Race. In 1933, the schooner Cape Race ran shore at Western Head near St. Shotts within sight of eight earlier wrecks.

An average of 158 foggy days per year, strong ocean currents, reefs and breakers, steep cliffs, ice and heavy seas have all taken their toll on ships venturing into these waters over the centuries. A shortage of lighthouses and foghorns, incomplete navigational charts and primitive equipment did nothing to improve the situation either. A look at a few of the shipwrecks might help paint at least a partial picture of Newfoundland's shipwreck history.

On June 4, 1883, the S. S. Texas ran aground at Mur Rock near St. Shotts with a motley cargo, which included 300 cattle, 1,406 sheep, 14,000 boxes of cheese, plus bacon, ham, flour, sole leather and nickel ore. Just two hours later, the S. S. Parkmore almost ran ashore in the same spot, saved only by the fact that the omnipresent fog had peeled back enough to allow those on board the Parkmore to see the wreck of the Texas.

All shipwrecks are tragic, but one of the most tragic was that of the Anglo Saxon off Cape Race on April 27, 1863. The Anglo Saxon had set sail from Liverpool, England on April 16, stopping in at Moville, Ireland to pick up some mail. Approaching the coast of Newfoundland, the ship ran into heavy ice and dense fog. Before long, the engines quit and the Anglo Saxon drifted slowly toward the shore, becoming loosely wedged between two rocks at a place called Clam Cove, north of Cape Race. The pounding seas shook the ship until the masts and rigging collapsed onto the terrified people below. All around, people clung desperately to bits and pieces of wreckage and screamed out for help. Some survivors made it to Cape Race in lifeboats; others were hauled up the nearby cliffs in baskets. The next day, the Dauntless out of St. John's as well as other smaller boats came to the scene and picked up some survivors found still clinging to the wreckage of the Anglo Saxon.

After most of the 209 survivors had returned to their homes (mostly in England), two children too young to know their own names remained behind in Newfoundland. The two were placed in the care of the St. John's Church of England Asylum for Widows and Orphans, while their photos were sent to the offices of the Allen Line in London, owners of the Anglo Saxon. The two children turned out to be Harriet Walton, age three, and her five-year-old brother, Edward Walton. They had been identified by their only living relative, a grandmother in East London. Their father had been a hairdresser, shoemaker and journeyman. Edward Walton later worked in a St. John's store, then moved to the United States. Harriet married and settled down in St. John's.

That so many of the Anglo Saxon's 446 passengers and crew survived is nothing short of a miracle. Most of the 237 people who died in the wreck had been passengers in the dank, crude steerage section of the ship. The bodies of more than 100 of these victims lie in unmarked graves at Clam Cove.

The Anglo Saxon disaster probably would not have

happened if the captain had not been foolhardy enough to nudge his ship close to the shore just to drop off a cannister of European newspapers, for which he reportedly was to receive fifty pounds. The tragedy prompted authorities to install a fog whistle at Cape Race and led to stricter regulations for the transport of passengers. Now, on a clear night, the automatic beacon of the Cape Race lighthouse flashes a signal which can be seen fifty miles out to sea.

Another earlier tragedy off Cape Race, on September 27, 1854, claimed 360 lives. Sixty-five miles off Cape Race, in thick fog, the American paddle steamer Arctic, enroute from Liverpool to New York, collided with the French steamer Vesta, bound for Quebec. The Arctic carried 250 passengers and a crew of 175; the Vesta had 147 passengers and fifty crewmembers.

Later, in an interview at St. John's, the Arctic's second officer Baalam reported that : "So dense was the fog that the other vessel could not be seen a minute before the collision. The wheel was put hard to starboard, the engine stopped immediately and reversed at full speed until we were clear of the other vessel. The French vessel seemed to be sinking bow first."

Drifting helplessly toward the shore, the disabled Arctic rammed into a boatload of people who had abandoned the Vesta; only one person, a woman, survived that collision. The Arctic went to the bottom, and 347 people lost their lives, including Captain Luce and his young son. Meanwhile, the Vesta, with 150 mattresses, as well as sails and planks lashed with cables over the huge hole in her bow, limped into St. John's, minus the unlucky thirteen who had died.

The wreck of the S. S. Florence near St. Shotts offers further proof, if such were needed, of the tragic record of shipwrecks along this stretch of coastline. The Florence, a steamer of the Furness line, set out from Halifax, enroute to St. John's with a load of Christmas merchandise. At around three o'clock in the morning darkness of December 20, 1912, after weaving her way through dangerous currents and breakers, the Florence ran aground on Saddleback Shoals.

The men crawled along the ship's bowsprit and scrambled onto icy ledges at the bottom of a 250-foot cliff, only to be lashed by a vicious rain and sleet storm. The captain then led his men back on board the ship, where he thought they might have a better chance at survival.

Second mate John Hedley decided to launch one of the lifeboats and go for help; four men volunteered to go with him. After rowing for about two miles, the men found a place to land. While trying to get ashore, two of the men were tossed overboard by the swell, but Hedley managed to drag them ashore, soaking wet but safe. After walking a ways, the men came upon a shack, which a man named James Bonia had built especially for any mariners who might be driven ashore at this God-forsaken spot. The shelter had food, firewood and matches, so the five men ate, then rested. Then Hedley and two men walked back to the cliff overlooking the Florence, but were unable to get a line to the men stranded on board the ship. They returned to the shelter to try to get some sleep. Before long, Hedley decided to check on the Florence again. This time, all he found of the ship was a mass of wreckage being tossed about by the angry sea. All eighteen men who had stayed on board the Florence had drowned, but the foresight of John Hedley and James Bonia had saved the lives of five men.

Then there's the story of the schooner Waterwitch. On November 29, 1875, the Waterwitch, on the way from St. John's to Cupids, rammed into the cliffs at a place called Horrid Gulch, not far from Pouch Cove near the northeastern tip of the Avalon Peninsula. It was late at night when the exhausted captain and two crew members of the Waterwitch made their way to Pouch Cove, where they roused a Mr. Langmead with news that some survivors of the shipwreck were huddled on ledges on the 600-foot-high cliffs. A man named Alfred Moores volunteered to lower himself down the cliff in the darkness and eventually found the survivors. Using ropes, Langmead and other residents of Pouch Cove dragged ten people up over the rocks to safety. For his part in the rescue, Alfred Moores received a silver watch from the people of St. John's and a silver medal from the Royal Humane Society, while other rescuers received bronze medals from the Royal Humane Society.

There have been suggestions that, at times, people on shore have flashed false signals to lure unsuspecting mariners to their doom, so that valuable food, clothing and other supplies could be salvaged. One old lady is reported to have hugged the captain of a wrecked ship and said, "Thank God for this happy blessing in bringing your ship on the land; now we have a stock of grub for the winter." She reportedly added, "The light on the cow's horns paid off."

No doubt many a ship's captain these days thanks God for better ships, improved navigating systems, more reliable weather forecasting, and residents who aren't as desperate for grub and other supplies as they once were.

PLACENTIA:
More Than A Pleasant Place

The story of Placentia fades into the mists and myths of history to around 1500, when the settlement was a major port for fishermen from western Europe. Yet, it wasn't until 1662 that the Government of France announced their official claim to Plaisance, meaning "pleasant place." And quite a pleasant spot Placentia is, sprawled on a flat, rocky stretch of beach jutting into Placentia Gut, and linked to the nearby town of Jerseyside by a lift-bridge constructed in 1960. Back in its early days, as many as 15,000 people lived here during the summer fishery. These days, the total population of Placentia and the surrounding communities is around 8,000. But, no matter what this place has lost in population, it still holds lots of charm.

Back in 1840, geologist J. B. Jukes provided an accurate, timeless description of the geography of Placentia, when he wrote of "bold cliffs and hills rising to a height of 400 to 500 feet extending into a shallow basin containing several islands and receiving a considerable brook." The "brook" Jukes referred to could have been either Northeast River or Southeast River, since both of these empty into separate inlets which merge at Placentia.

One of the earliest maps of Newfoundland, drafted in 1541, designated the tiny Placentia peninsula as "Insulace Corte Realis", suggesting that explorers Miguel and Gaspar Corte Real may have claimed the area for the Portuguese Government. A 1547 Spanish map showed "Isle de Plaziencia". More than two centuries later, Captain James Cook drew up a detailed map of the whole of Placentia Bay.

In 1660, King Louis of France appointed Nicholas Gargot "Count of Placentia, Chevalier of Our Order of Saint Michael, Marshal of the Armies, Captain of Ships", and ordered him to seize and fortify Grand and Little Placentia (the latter now Argentia, site of an American military base). Sailing into Placentia on board the Leopard, Gargot found sixteen Basque ships and seven Spanish ships there. The fishermen protested and eventually forced Gargot to move to a less hostile colony in Quebec.

Two years later, Gargot sent Le Sieur de Perron with fifty colonists to join the twenty-man garrison already at Placentia. That winter, thirteen of the colonists, including de Perron, were killed in drunken skirmishes. The ringleaders of the uprising were shipped off to Quebec and executed; Gargot then sent another twenty soldiers to Placentia.

In 1667, to encourage people to settle at Placentia, King Louis offered ships' masters a hundred dollars for each man and sixty dollars for each woman transported to the colony. When Sieur de la Palme took charge of the colony in December of that year he counted sixty families and 150 soldiers at Placentia.

The residents complained of unjust treatment under de la Palme and, in 1670, the governor was recalled to France. The new governor, Sieur de la Poippe, arrived later that year and found the community tightly controlled by the all-powerful fishing admirals. Although his governship of Placentia lasted some fifteen years, Poippe, too, was highly unpopular, with settlers accusing him of dispensing supplies and prized beach frontage in an unfair way.

The fishery of 1680 was a dismal failure, followed by a drastic decline in the French population at Placentia. In an effort to protect the dwindling French population from being outnumbered by other nationalities, the Government of France revoked Basque and Spanish fishing rights in the area. That year, Sieur de Parat replaced Poippe as governor of Placentia.

In 1686, the Recollect Fathers built the first church at Placentia, on the site of the present Anglican Church. The fishery of 1687 was a good one for the 256 people then living at Placentia. But the town had little protection from attack; Fort Louis had eight cannons and no ammunition. In August, three ships arrived at Placentia with twenty-five soldiers and twelve new cannons.

Governor Parat proved to be unpopular among the citizens of Placentia because of his unfairness and immorality – he had brought a Parisian woman named de l'Isle as his mistress. After sustained pressure from the Church, Madame de l'Isle and her children were shipped back to France. But the conflict between the Church and the Government persisted, finally exploding in the riots of 1690. At around the same time, forty-five English pirates captured the town and the garrison, threw the cannons into the sea and made off with two stolen French ships loaded with valuables.

PLACENTIA

On September 15, 1692, five English ships and 600 men launched an attack on what is now Freshwater, not far from Placentia. The French stood their ground, and, after blasting Fort Louis for five hours, the English attackers sailed away.

The French - English War raged from 1694 to 1714. During that time, the English made several unsuccessful attempts to take Placentia, which, by now, was very well fortified. The clashes finally came to an end in 1713, when the Treaty of Utrecht forced France to abandon Placentia, while pledging not to set up another colony on the island of Newfoundland.

Not long after, Queen Anne of England gave permission for Protestants to own land at Placentia. As a result, quite a few British settlers bought land from the French, who were leaving Placentia in droves.

Around 1717, Colonel Gledhill was appointed commander of the fort at Placentia and lieutenant-governor of the town. For some raeson, Gledhill did not arrive at Placentia until 1719, when he found the settlers living in poverty. From 1713 to 1729, Placentia was under the jurisdiction of Nova Scotia and the fishing admirals in the area regularly tested Gledhill's authority.

Finally, in 1729, justices were appointed to the colony at Placentia and the first Anglican clergyman was stationed there. The fishing and shipbuilding industries prospered. One Placentia shipbuilder, John Phillips, turned to fishing, and later to piracy on the high seas.

In 1729, Gledhill handed over control of Placentia to Otto Hamilton, who served until 1757. During Hamilton's term, Placentia could boast that one-fifth of all the ships in Newfoundland waters sailed from this sheltered port; Irish immigrants flocked to the area, which still has many surnames from the Emerald Isle.

On August 1, 1749, Hamilton reported that three invalids, four deserters, 107 privates, seven officers, sixteen military men, three drummers and ten mistresses were then living at Placentia.

A report prepared for the British Government early in the eighteenth century described Placentia as "the only port in the whole of America whence the French can obtain dried cod in time of war, since the other places are open harbours, without fortifications".

The French began construction of Fort Royal on a hill overlooking Placentia in 1693. That citadel became one of the most important defence installations in the area. One British soldier imprisoned there reported that the walls were sixteen feet high and eighteen feet thick,

Placentia Calvin Coish

although another British source said the fort was poorly constructed. Excavations at the site uncovered outer walls of stone eight feet thick, and inner walls two feet thick, with earth and rubble between. The British took over Fort Royal in 1713 and renamed it Castle Hill; they abandoned the site in 1811. Today, it is preserved as a National Historic Site, with Fort Royal, the Detached Redoubt, le Gaillardin and La Fontaine Battery mere remnants of their former glory days when the French ruled Placentia.

Fort Frederick, built by the British, has also been buried under the dust of centuries. The only indication that a fort ever existed on this spot is a plaque, with an inscription which reads in part: "A fort consisting of a semi-circular redoubt mounting twelve guns, a guardhouse, barracks and storehouse surrounded by a palisade was erected on this site in 1721 and was named after Prince Frederick, then Prince of Wales."

One of the first conservation laws in North America was enacted at Placentia in 1779 by Prince William Henry, who declared: "People are strictly forbidden to destroy the birds on the coast and adjacent islands except for food and bait. And if any persons are found offending, they will be apprehended and sent to St. John's in order to be tried for this offence, and the feathers found in their custody will be seized and confiscated."

For centuries, fishing was the economic mainstay of the Placentia area. The Second World War changed that, when the Americans opened a naval base at nearby Argentia, bringing extra employment and economic security. In 1956, 872 people worked at the Argentia base. As this chapter was being written, the American Government was accelerating plans to shut down the operation, putting the final 265 people employed there out of work.

Some of the history of the Placentia area is being preserved in the local museum, which officially opened in the summer of 1976. The museum features such items as Prince William Henry's tipstaff, the 1800 commission of Lieutenant Edward Collins, Royal Navy, a document signed by Louis XIV granting Point Verde to Governor Sieur de Constabelle, a roster of residents who defended Placentia against the pirate attack of 1794, and a colourful quilt put together by women of the Jerseyside Jubilee Guild in the 1930s to help recreate just a slice of the rich historical mosaic of the Placentia area.

Roman Catholic Church at Placentia Calvin Coish

CARBONEAR:
Newfoundland's Gibraltar

Lots o' fish in Bonavis' Harbour,
Lots o' fish all down around here,
Boys and girls are fishin' together
Forty-five from Carbonear.

    Carbonear. The name summons visions of fishing admirals, buccaneers and an assortment of other characters, and perhaps even romance. The most likely derivation of the name is from the French word charbonnier, meaning charcoal-burner.

    Fishing admirals who visited Newfoundland in the middle of the sixteenth century made reference to the port and, in 1614, the pirate Peter Easton is reported to have captured a French salt ship in the harbour. By 1627 there were twenty-two houses in Carbonear. Today, this community of some 5,000 people, nestled in a protected indraft of Conception Bay, sixty-five miles from St. John's, is an important commercial and service centre for the area.

    At the mouth of the harbour stands Carbonear Island,

guarding the entrance like a sentinel. In 1679, English settlers constructed a fort on this island. During the harsh winter of 1696-97, the French pillaged settlements all over the Avalon Peninsula, and burned the twenty-two houses then standing at Carbonear. Residents fled to Carbonear Island and, from there, successfully fought off the French attackers. According to French reports at the time, Carbonear had the best-built houses in Newfoundland and was the home of some very wealthy merchants.

In 1705, residents again retreated to Carbonear Island and beat off another French attack. The island was garrisoned and defended by a militia of fishermen in 1745. Old cannons from those days still stand defiantly on Harbour Rock Hill in the centre of town. When American privateers attacked Carbonear in 1755, residents again took to Carbonear Island and fought off the invaders. Only once did French forces take the island; that was in 1762.

One historian noted that, "except for the two successful defences of Carbonear Island, the French roamed at will throughout English Newfoundland with little fear of retaliation." Little wonder then that Carbonear Island became known as the "Gibraltar of Newfoundland."

From 1745 to 1750, the Carbonear area had a garrison consisting of one officer of artillery, twenty artillery men, one officer on foot, twenty soldiers, and 200 small arms for use by citizens.

It was only fitting that, on June 1, 1981, the Canadian Government declared Carbonear Island (and the courthouse at nearby Harbour Grace) National Historic Sites. At the same time, the town officially opened Carbonear Memorial Park on the waterfront to honour the dead of two world wars. A granite tower in the park pays tribute to postmistress Tryphoena Nicholl, who died after saving the lives of two people during a fire which destroyed the post office on the night of June 25, 1904. One of the two people saved was Rev. Dr. Levi Curtis, who was in town on business and asleep on the top floor of the building when the fire broke out.

Until the recent ban on codfishing, Carbonear had relied heavily on the fishery for its economic stability. Sealing too was an integral part of the town's reliance on the ocean. For example, in 1824, more than 100,000 seal pelts were landed there. In 1836, eighty ships and 2,000 men sailed from Carbonear in search of seals.

Carbonear has produced its fair share of shipbuilders, sailors, fishermen, sealers and merchants. One such interesting character was Captain Frank Taylor, who sailed from Carbonear, en route to Oporto, Portugal in 1837 with a load of codfish. Taylor's plan was to sail from Oporto, straight to the seal herds off Newfoundland. Before he even reached Portugal, Taylor was forced to take an unexpected detour after French soldiers boarded the Providence, which they mistook for a pirate ship, and proudly escorted their catch to Bordeaux.

Taylor contacted the British consul there and laid out his story. Luckily, the consul believed Taylor and released him, his ship and crew. Taylor then set out for Oporto, sold his fish for a tidy profit and sailed back across the Atlantic to get in on the seal hunt. Off Green Bay, Taylor and his men came upon a herd of seals and loaded up with more than 5,000 pelts. The Providence sailed through the Narrows of St. John's to the boom of guns and the rousing cheers of hundreds of onlookers. In recognition of the feat, the St. John's Chamber of

Commerce gave Taylor and his crew its cherished silk flag.

Captain Giles of Carbonear was supposedly the first sealing captain to prohibit the killing of seals on the Sabbath. More than once, we are told, Giles' strict observance of Sunday would be rewarded when, the following day, while other ships were jammed solid in the ice, a clear channel would open up for Giles' ship to pass through with little problem.

Michael Kearney was a famous shipbuilder from Carbonear. In 1852, John Rorke and Sons launched the Thomas Ridley, a 170-ton vessel Kearney had constructed. When he died, Kearney was building the Shamrock, the last square-rigger constructed at Carbonear. After Kearney's death, Richard Horwood completed construction of the Shamrock.

One of the most touching stories from Carbonear's colourful history is that of the Irish princess, Sheila Na Geira, daughter of the King of County Down, Ireland. During the reign of Elizabeth I, Princess Sheila was taken captive in the English Channel by a pirate named Gilbert Pike, who had earlier broken ranks with pirate Peter Easton, reportedly over the division of booty. Pike brought the princess across the Atlantic with him. We are told that Pike fell in love with the dark-haired beauty and she feel in love with him and convinced him to give up his unsavoury trade. They settled at a place called Bristol's Hope, near Harbour Grace. Today, a huge tombstone in a garden at the west end of Carbonear stands near what many assume to be the remains of the pirate and the princess, who lived to be 105 years old.

Recalled in a less romantic vein is the winter of 1816, when angry mobs roared through the town, looting stores. That winter became known as "The Winter of the Rals (Riots)." Equally black is Old Christmas Day, 1862, when mummers went on a rampage and shot Magistrate McNeill. Police had to be called in from St. John's and the nearby town of Harbour Grace.

The Churches have long been a central part in the life and culture of Carbonear. The history of the Roman Catholic, Anglican and United Church ministries in the town goes back to the latter part of the eighteenth century. The present St. Patrick's Church was built in 1891. St. James Anglican Church, a wooden building on Bond Street, dates back to the 1860s. Bethany United Church was built in the mid-1960s to replace a building constructed in 1874. The Salvation Army opened their Citadel at Carbonear in 1953.

Of course, with the Churches came schools. In the 1800s, a private school at Carbonear looked after the needs of the girls of "respectable" families. In 1838, the Newfoundland Legislature passed an act to establish a grammar school at Carbonear. On October 15, 1905, Governor McGregor laid the cornerstone of the new Methodist Grammar School in the town. The Church of England opened St. James School on November 25, 1908. Today, Carbonear has modern schools that rank with the best in the province. The town also has a community college campus, an industrial park, shopping malls and recreational facilities.

The new eight-storey hospital at Carbonear was opened in the fall of 1976. The old hospital, built in 1957, had fifty-two beds; the new building has 135 beds and a staff of 200.

Carbonear has been home to a number of newspapers, such as *The Star*, which began publication in January, 1833. On May 22, 1879, John Rochefort began publishing the weekly *Carbonear Herald*. M. J. Walker started *The Weekly News* on November 16, 1892. In recent years, *The Compass* has earned a reputation as a fine community newspaper.

The community of Freshwater touches the town of Carbonear and has long been considered part of it. Just a short hop inland is Victoria, settled by farmers in the early 1800s. Some people will tell you they're from Victoria, B. C. - Victoria, Back of Carbonear, that is. The stands of fir and birch which grew in the area came in handy for making barrel hoops and staves and produced lumber for local merchants and shipbuilders. The trees aren't as thick as they once were, but the people are still here, taking pride in their community, the Gibraltar of Newfoundland.

The Carbonear waterfront   Bill Bowman

NEWFOUNDLAND:
Trans-Atlantic Stepping Stone

On a sunny morning late in July, 1978, Major Christopher Davey and Donald Cameron lifted off from Bannerman Park, St. John's in their nine-storey, yellow balloon. The two adventurers were hoping to be the first to cross the Atlantic Ocean by balloon – almost an anomaly in this age of supersonic travel. They probably would have made it if the helium hadn't seeped out of their craft, forcing them to ditch just a hundred miles short of the coast of Brittany.

The attempt by Cameron and Davey was soon overshadowed by the feat of three Americans who had lifted off from Maine, then drifted over the Atlantic, landing in France, about sixty miles from where Lindbergh had touched down more than fifty years before.

If it did nothing else, the attempt by Cameron and Davey to cross the Atlantic helped highlight Newfoundland's place in aviation history. Waiting in St. John's for more than three weeks for just the right weather conditions, the two balloonists took some time to learn about this province's role in the history of flight.

They chatted with a St. John's salesman who recalled seeing Lindbergh's plane, The Spirit of St. Louis, fly over St. John's on May 20, 1927. Lindbergh had taken off from Roosevelt Field in New York eleven hours earlier. Twenty-two and a half hours after exciting the people of St. John's, he landed at Le Bourget Airport near Paris and became the first person to fly alone across the Atlantic.

The heated race to be the first across the Atlantic by air started almost ten years after the Wright brothers made their brief flight at Kitty Hawk on December 17, 1903. In April of 1913, Lord Northcliffe, publisher of the London *Daily Mail,* offered the generous prize of 10,000 pounds (around $50,000) "to the first person who crosses the Atlantic from any point in the United States, Canada or Newfoundland to any point in Great Britain or Ireland in seventy-two continuous hours."

First to make plans to go after the prize was British pilot, Lieutenant John Cyril Porte with the America, a flying boat designed by American Glenn Curtiss, archrival of the Wright brothers. Curtiss planned to have Porte fly the America to Newfoundland for the official start of the flight, stop at the Azores to refuel, then fly on to Britain. To boost his chances of striking good weather, Porte would have to leave Newfoundland by August 15. But, the year was 1914 and on August 4, before Porte had a chance to get started, Britain declared war on Germany and Porte signed up with the Royal Navy.

The war soon made flying boats like the America obsolete, so Curtiss, with the help of the United States Navy, drafted plans for a new aircraft, a seaplane bomber. In January, 1918, work began on the Navy Curtiss aircraft or NCs (later nicknamed Nancies). The four-engine NCs had a wingspan of 126 feet and measured more than sixty-eight feet from nose tip to tail.

In November, 1918, the war came to an end and the Nancies were no longer needed as bombers. Lord Northcliffe renewed his pre-war offer of a generous reward for the first trans-Atlantic flight. Reports suggest that the United States Navy secretly planned a go at the prize. Meanwhile, a number of British airmen were making their own preparations.

Four British teams decided to try flying west to east to take advantage of the prevailing westerlies and shipped their planes to Newfoundland. First to arrive in St. John's was the Atlantic, a Sopwith aircraft, to be piloted by Harry Hawker, with Lieutenant-Commander Kenneth MacKenzie-Grieve to act as navigator.

Reaching St. John's on March 29, 1919, Hawker and Grieve found out that the prime take-off spot had been reserved by another team, F. P. Raynham and C. W. F. Morgan, whose Martinsyde aircraft, named the Raymor, reached St. John's in April. Next came the Handley-Page V/1500, a four engine bomber with a four-man crew and a wingspan of 126 feet. Last to arrive in the Newfoundland capital was the Vickers-Vimy of Captain John Alcock and Lieutenant Arthur Whitten-Brown.

In the meantime, three NCs had arrived at Trepassey Bay, some sixty miles south of St. John's. The Americans had even gone so far as to position sixty ships across the Atlantic to assist in their efforts. The Yanks also dispatched a C-5 blimp to St. John's, and anchored it near Quidi Vidi Lake. On May 15, a strong wind ripped the blimp from its moorings and sent it drifting out over the Atlantic. The crew had just enough time to jump to safety and one of them broke an ankle.

After several unsuccessful attempts to get in the air, three NCs lifted off from Trepassey Bay, bound for the

DISTANT SHORES

Cameron and Davey lift off from Bannerman Park, July 26, 1978

Calvin Coish

Azores. Two days later, the British fliers at St. John's were still socked in by bad weather. Over the Atlantic, the NCs ran into dense fog. One NC touched down on the Atlantic to get its bearings and was damaged beyond repair. The Greek ship Ionia picked up the crew. Meanwhile, the NC-4, which had been plagued with engine trouble, had reached the Azores, while the NC-3 had been forced down forty-five miles to the west.

The British in St. John's had no idea what was happening to the Nancies and were pressing on with their own plans. On May 18, Hawker and Grieve lifted off from Glendenning's Farm west of St. John's and swung their craft, the Atlantic, east over the broad expanse of ocean. A week later, the world learned that Hawker and Grieve had ditched in the ocean a few hundred miles out of St. John's and a Danish trawler had rescued them. The wreckage of their plane was salvaged and put on display in England.

Absorbed by the attempt by Hawker and Grieve, the British hardly noticed what happened next. The NC-4, commanded by Putty Read, stopped over in the Azores, took off again, and landed at Lisbon, Portugal almost ten hours later, completing the first trans-Atlantic crossing by air.

Undeterred, in the early afternoon of Saturday, June 14, 1919, Alcock and Brown took off from Lester's Field in the west end of St. John's. Almost immediately, their radio went dead, cutting them off from weather forecasts and other vital communications. Sitting in their open cockpit, lashed by wind and rain, the two aviators pushed on. At eight-thirty the next morning, they sighted the coast of Ireland. With visibility low, they decided to bring their plane down in a clearing, which turned out to be a bog near Clifden, Ireland. The

Vickers-Vimy scuffed and bounced along, coming to a halt nose down in the mushy peat. Despite their inelegant landing, Alcock and Brown had made the first non-stop aerial crossing of the Atlantic; they were later knighted for their achievement.

In November, 1952, the Canadian Government put up a concrete monument about a mile from Lester's Field, at the corner of Patrick Street and LeMarchant Road. Farther west along LeMarchant Road, at Lester's Field, Premier Joey Smallwood unveiled another monument in 1969, to mark the fiftieth anniversary of the flight by Alcock and Brown.

Rather than acting as a deterrent, the success of Alcock and Brown only spurred others to try their luck at crossing the Atlantic. On July 4, the Handley-Page lifted off at Harbour Grace and promptly fell back to the ground again. Not one of the four-man crew was injured.

Between May 23 and June 11, 1927, three Italians in the Santa Maria II made the first trans-Atlantic return flight between Trepassey Bay and Lisbon. On September 7 of that year, James Victor Medcalf and Terrance Bernard Tully took off from Harbour Grace in the Sir John Carling. It was the last anyone was to hear of the unlucky aviators. On April 12 and 13, 1928, Hermann Koehl, James Fitzmaurice and G. von Huenefeld made the first non-stop east to west flight from Baldonnel, Ireland to Greely Island, Labrador in the Bremen, a Junkers aircraft.

Then there was Amelia Earhart, nicknamed Lady Lindy. On Sunday, June 17, 1928, Earhart, accompanied by Wilmer Stultz and Louis Gordon, took off from Trepassey. The next day they brought the Friendship down near Port Burry, Wales, and Earhart went into the history books as the first woman to fly across the Atlantic. In May of 1932, Earhart topped that achievement when she flew from Harbour Grace to Culmore, Northern Ireland and became the first woman to make a solo aerial crossing of the Atlantic.

The list of people willing to risk their lives trying to fly across the stormy Atlantic goes on and on and reads like a veritable calendar of great moments in early aviation. Harbour Grace, St. John's and Trepassey were the usual takeoff and landing spots.

On October 17, 1928, for instance, H. C. MacDonald set out from St. John's in a de Havilland aircraft, the Gypsy Moth, and was never heard from again. On October 22, 1929, U. Diteman took off from Harbour Grace in the Golden Hind and flew to his doom. In 1930, C. S. Wynn-Eaton crashed while taking off at Harbour Grace and escaped with minor injuries. On August of the same year, J. Brown and H. Mears tried to take off at Harbour Grace in their Lockheed Vega, called the City of New York. They had a tire blowout and crashed, but there were no serious injuries. On October 9, J. Errol Boyd and Harry P. Connor set out from Harbour Grace in the Maple Leaf en route to Berlin. They made it as far as the Isles of Scilly, in England.

On June 24, 1931, Otto Hillig and Holger Hoiriis took off from Harbour Grace in the Liberty, bound for Copenhagen, Denmark. The next day they came down at Krefeld, Germany. On July 15 of that year, Hungarian fliers Alexander Magyar and Gyorgy Endres left Harbour Grace in the Justice For Hungary, hoping to reach Budapest. They landed instead at Bicske, Hungary.

On May 13, 1932, L. Reichers set out from Harbour Grace in the Liberty. Engine trouble forced him down about fifty miles from Ireland. On August 23 of that year, Carl Petersen and Thor Solberg crashed while trying to land at Darby's Harbour and walked away uninjured. Two days later, Clyde A. Lee and John Bochkon headed off from Harbour Grace in the Green Mountain Boy, never to be seen again.

On August 8, 1933, Joseph and Benjamin Adamowicz and Emil Bergin took off from New York in the White Eagle, hoping to make it to Warsaw, Poland. Instead, they crash-landed safely at Harbour Grace.

Between August 22 and September 6, 1934, R. Light and R. Wilson few from Cartwright, Labrador to Edinburgh, Scotland in the Asulinak, en route to Manila.

In the summer of 1935, Thor Solberg and Paul Oscanyan flew from Cartwright to Bergen, Norway, stopping at Greenland, Iceland and the Faeroe Islands along the way.

In 1936, Henry T. Merrill and Harry Richman took off from Harbour Grace in the Lady Peace, bound for London, England. They got as far as Llandilo, Wales. On a return flight from Birkdale, they were forced down by weather at Musgrave Harbour on September 14. On October 29, James Mollison made his first west to east crossing from Harbour Grace to Croydon, England in the Dorothy.

On July 5 and 6, 1937, H. Gray and his crew flew from Botwood to Foynes, Ireland in a Sikorsky S-42, the Clipper III, on a commercial survey flight for Pan American Airways.

On May 16, 1939, Carl Backman set out from Gander in the Monocoupe 90-A and was never heard from again.

An exhibit at Gander International Airport records some of these milestones in trans-Atlantic aviation. It's nice to know that we haven't lost touch with the critical role this province played in that story.

FERRYLAND:
Baltimore's Place

Back in 1620, an Englishman, Sir George Calvert, who later assumed the title Lord Baltimore, purchased a Newfoundland land claim from his friend, Sir William Vaughan. Baltimore called his new province Avalon, in honour of the supposed birthplace of Christianity in England, and set up his headquarters at Ferryland, a cozy little harbour some forty miles south of St. John's.

Exactly how Ferryland got its name is a matter of some debate. Some say the name is a variation of the English Veralum, an early name of St. Alban's in England. Others say the name comes from the Portuguese word for rocky. The most plausible theory is that Ferryland gets its name from the French word forillon, which means "standing out or separated from the mainland," an apt description of the little peninsula known as Ferryland Downs which juts out into the Atlantic Ocean. While there may be some disagreement about the origin of Ferryland's name, there is no disputing the rich history of this community.

There are indications that French fishermen visited

Ferryland as early as 1504. Each year the French would set up their summer fishing stations along the south coast of Newfoundland, where the fishery would begin a month earlier than along the iceberg-prone east coast.

The town's first permanent settlers – a dozen of them – arrived at Ferryland on September 5, 1621, accompanied by Captain Edward Wynne, whom Lord Baltimore had sent to govern the new colony. By Christmas, the settlers had built a house and, by spring, had completed a forge and salt works, dug a well sixteen feet deep, and built a seven-foot-high palisade around the settlement. In 1622, Captain Daniel Powell brought twenty-two new settlers, including seven women, to the colony.

Despite the glowing reports Wynne sent back to

Ferryland Downs Lighthouse   Nfld. Dept. of Development

England, Lord Baltimore began to suspect that things in the new colony weren't quite as rosy as Wynne suggested. Baltimore also suspected that Wynne and Powell were creaming off a substantial part of the thousands of pounds he was investing in the colony each year. In 1626, Baltimore sent Sir Arthur Ashton to Ferryland to take over from Wynne. Finally, in 1627, having put some 60,000 pounds into the colony, Baltimore decided to step in and take direct control of Ferryland, arriving there on July 23. Baltimore stayed for only six weeks, but he was impressed enough to come back the next year with his wife and children, except for his oldest son, Cecil.

Under Baltimore's direction the colony appeared to prosper. Baltimore even managed to work out some heated differences betwen his Catholic and Protestant settlers. Things were going along fine until French warships attacked the colony and captured several fishing boats, crews and supplies. Baltimore struck back with his own forces and seized six French ships at Trepassey, about forty miles south of Ferryland.

By the following winter, things weren't going nearly as well for the fledgling community. The settlers found the soil hard to cultivate and the winter weather cold and harsh. The food supply dwindled and disease spread through the colony. The climate turned out to be especially rough for Lady Baltimore's sensitive health, so, with her children, she sailed south to the new settlement at Jamestown, Virginia. The following summer, in desperation, Baltimore wrote to King Charles I of England: "I am determined to commit this place to fishermen that are able to encounter storms and hard weather, and to remove myself, with some forty persons, to Your Majesty's Dominion of Virginia, where, if Your

Majesty will please to grant me a precinct of land, with such privileges as the King, Your Father, My Gracious Majesty, was pleased to grant me here, I shall endeavour to the utmost of my power to preserve it."

Baltimore did in fact follow his family to Virginia, but records indicate that the settlers there gave him a rather icy reception, largely because, as a Roman Catholic, he refused to sign an oath of supremacy in the United States. The King recalled Baltimore to England. His wife and children followed but were lost at sea.

Exactly what happened next has been muddied by the years. Some historians contend that Baltimore did receive a charter for a tract of land in America; others say he died while waiting for the King to approve his application. At any rate, it seems that Lord Baltimore never did return to America, and the charter for Maryland went to his son, Cecil, who became the second Lord Baltimore.

While the historic connection between Ferryland and Maryland has been largely overlooked, it has been enshrined in the Great Seal of Maryland, which bears the inscription (translated from the Latin): "Cecilius, Absolute Lord of Maryland and Avalon, Baron of Baltimore." On the reverse side of the seal, the Baltimore coat of arms is flanked by two figures – one a Maryland planter, the other a Newfoundland fisherman. Indeed, then Maryland Governor Spiro T. Agnew, who later became Vice-President of the United States, declared September 20, 1967 to be Maryland-Ferryland Day.

At Ferryland, the first Lord Baltimore constructed a majestic stone mansion, which he called Mansion House, reportedly the largest such dwelling in North America at the time. Even earlier, around 1612, the pirate Peter Easton made Ferryland his headquarters and built a mansion on Fox Hill. Today, unfortunately, there is no sign of either Baltimore's or Easton's house.

After the death of his father, Cecil Calvert kept the colony of Avalon going and continued to appoint governors to run it. But it seems that the second Lord Baltimore devoted most of his time and energy to developing the new Maryland colony. Eventually, the job of maintaining Ferryland fell to Sir David Kirke, who moved there in 1638 under a royal charter and occupied Baltimore's mansion.

The resourceful Kirke supervised the construction of forts at Bay Bulls, St. John's and Ferryland and managed the thriving settlement at Ferryland. He sold fishing licences, rented fishing premises, and charged all foreign fishermen a tax of five fish for every 120 they caught. Kirke brought more fishermen from England and issued licences to tavernkeepers.

Like Baltimore, Kirke was a staunch Royalist. During the struggle between King Charles I and Parliament (as a result of which Charles literally lost his head), Kirke offered the King refuge at Ferryland – an offer the King turned down. Kirke even made plans to invade England in support of Charles, but these plans came to nothing. Oliver Cromwell and his supporters won out and summoned Kirke to England to answer charges of insurrection. Because Kirke had not actually taken up arms, he was allowed to return to Newfoundland, but Cromwell later sent a British fleet to dismantle Ferryland's defences. Some say Kirke returned to England, where he died in 1654; others say he died at Ferryland in 1655 and was buried on the Downs.

In 1661, the new King of England ordered that the Province of Avalon be restored to Baltimore's newly-appointed governor, Robert Swanley. For a while,

Ferryland continued to prosper, until it came under assault from French and Dutch ships. In 1673 Dutch forces attacked and burned much of the settlement, including the Kirke plantation.

Like many Newfoundland communities, Ferryland was many times caught up in skirmishes, especially between English and French forces. In 1694, for example, Captain William Holman and his men fought for five hours using only thirty guns to successfully beat off an attack from more heavily armed French troops. Two years later, the settlers weren't so lucky when the French commander d'Iberville captured the town and used it as a base in launching a murderous attack against St. John's and other communities on the Avalon Peninsula. Probably the most famous battle in Ferryland's history took place in 1762 when Robert Carter and his wife led a successful defence against French warships bombarding the colony.

The 1762 battle might well have gone the other way if the people of Ferryland had not petitioned the government about forty years earlier to fortify their town. In response to that request, Captain Thomas Smith placed eight of his ship's cannons at the southern tip of Isle aux Bois, just off Ferryland harbour, and four others on the western side of the harbour. Smith also built a powder magazine and barracks to house twenty soldiers. Between 1746 and 1749 the island's defences were strengthened even more.

The Ferryland Museum, which at various times has served as a bank, a jail, a courthouse, and a home, preserves some of the area's local history by displaying a variety of items, many on loan from local residents. Here you might see a chair and silverware from the Florizel, which sank off Cappahayden in 1918, a washstand from another wrecked ship, the Christiana, killicks, old lanterns, and a wooden grub box.

Still, there has been little effort to mine the mother lode of history which practically seeps from the rocks and hills and gentle slopes around Ferryland. There is little to suggest that the coarse talk and raucous laughter of pirates, generals, soldiers and humble fisherfolk once echoed over the mist-covered Downs. It is indeed a pity that the Canadian and Newfoundland governments have not seen fit to restore the Ferryland of Baltimore and Kirke and Easton, complete with forts, barracks, cannons and stately mansions. Restored to even a shade of its former splendour, Ferryland could rival the renewed grandeur of Louisbourg or Annapolis Royal or King's Landing.

NEWFOUNDLAND'S PIRATES:
The Jolly Roger and Pieces of Eight

What is the common thread which links places like Harbour Grace, Brigus, Ferryland, Kelligrews, Kelly's Island, Sandy Point and Turk's Gut? Students of Newfoundland history will recognize that all these places have some connection, whether solid or tenuous, with the pirates who, for centuries, pillaged and terrorized ships and settlements along the Newfoundland coast.

Ask almost any Newfoundlander to name a pirate and he'll most likely respond quick as a flash: "Peter Easton". Easton, probably our most infamous pirate, was a bold swashbuckler who, for two years, plied his evil trade along the Newfoundland coast and into the Caribbean. Easton's career as a pirate started around 1602, when the English government sent him to escort a fishing fleet across the Atlantic. They were barely out of port, when Easton spotted a Dutch pirate ship and came up with other ideas. Easton and his men promptly seized the

Dutch vessel, which carried the passengers of a captured Irish ship.

Easton came to Harbour Grace around 1610 with a fleet of ten armed ships. He built a fort and pressed fishermen into serving with him (although it's said that many joined his lucrative trade willingly) and took to capturing and looting ships and settlements. The king of pirates operated in style, often taking minstrels and trumpeters with him to herald his arrival. In Conception Bay, Easton seized two ships and a hundred men, sparing the town of Cupids after the settlers gave him two pigs. At St. John's, Easton captured thirty ships. On one occasion, he was even bold enough to capture the governor of Newfoundland, Richard Whitbourne, and held him captive for eleven days. Ironically, Whitbourne had been sent to Newfoundland to try to bring some semblance of law and order to a system ruled by pirates and fishing admirals.

It was September, 1611, and the most feared and most fearless pirate in the world was sailing towards Harbour Grace, bringing the San Sebastian, loaded with treasure from Spanish America. Just outside the harbour, the French fleet, headed by the St. Malo, waited. Through clever seamanship and manoeuvering of his ships, Easton and his men defeated the French fleet and sent the St. Malo crashing to her doom on a small island which became known as "Easton's Isle." It's said that forty-seven men killed in that skirmish lie buried at Bear Cove near Harbour Grace.

Some reports suggest that Easton had a fort on Kelly's Island in Conception Bay. That island, it's been suggested, gets its name from another pirate who lived there and held off other privateers by tricking them with wooden cannons installed at various points around the small island. There are rumours that, some years ago, American treasure-hunters made off with a fortune in coins they found on Kelly's Island.

The town of Kelligrews in Conception Bay apparently gets its name from a Cornish family who exerted influence in the courts of Queen Elizabeth I and her successor, James I. It is said that, while serving royalty, the Kelligrews (or Killigrews) were also hard at work fitting out pirates and privateers at the English ports of Falmouth and Poole.

Eventually, English merchants, fed up with the great losses they were suffering at the hands of pirates, most notably Peter Easton, petitioned Lord Admiral Nottingham to catch the man who had become known variously as "the Great Easton", "the Pirate Admiral", and "the Arch-Pirate". In response, Nottingham chose young Navy Captain Henry Mainwaring to lead a fleet in search of Easton. Not satisfied with the inadequate fleet Nottingham had given him, Mainwaring outfitted a better fleet at his own expense and, at the age of 23, sailed the waters around England in search of Easton.

The delay in Mainwaring's preparations gave the Kelligrews time to warn Easton, who then phased out his pirate activities off the coast of Europe and headed across the Atlantic. Powerful as he was, and easily a match for Mainwaring, Easton still had no desire to possibly one day face charges of high treason against the English Crown. So, while Mainwaring was still searching for him in the waters around Britain, Easton was busy building a fort at Harbour Grace.

Frustrated in his attempts to capture Easton, Mainwaring received royal assent to seize Spanish ships bringing back riches from the Aztec and Inca civilizations. Mainwaring set up his headquarters on the

Barbary Coast of the Mediterranean, still harbouring plans to pursue Easton later. Mainwaring grew rich and gathered a powerful fleet in preparation for the capture of the greatest pirate of them all.

Easton got word of Mainwaring's growing strength and moved his headquarters from Harbour Grace to Ferryland on the southern shore of the Avalon Peninsula. From Ferryland, Easton continued to plunder ships which dared to sail anywhere from the North Atlantic to the Caribbean. On one occasion, he sailed into San Juan, Puerto Rico and took the governor's palace, something Sir Francis Drake had tried to do thirteen years earlier but without success. Further enhanced by that bold act, Easton's reputation took on legendary dimensions.

Nevertheless, just to be on the safe side and in good graces where it counted most, Easton asked King James I of England for a pardon. We are told that the pardon was granted - twice - but we have no indication that Easton ever had need of it. After he retired from his years of piracy, Easton moved to France, married a rich woman and spent the rest of his life in luxury as the Marquis of Savoy.

Meanwhile, Mainwaring came to Newfoundland in 1614, took over Easton's abandoned forts, and, for three months, carried out his own raids on vessels which ventured into the waters around Newfoundland. Mainwaring reported that he never had the slightest difficulty getting men to join his crew of their own accord. In fact, when he left Newfoundland 500 men went with him.

Mainwaring went back to England, shared his wealth with the king and received a full royal pardon. He became an admiral of the fleet and, in the ultimate irony of ironies, turned out pamphlets condemning the evils of piracy. He even gained a seat in the British Parliament.

George Pearcival, a fish salter from Placentia Bay, got his first taste of the pirate's trade on board an English ship bound for South America when the whole crew, including the captain, turned to piracy. Pearcival ended up back home in Great Paradise, longing for the day when the salty fish would no longer sting his calloused hands. On a foggy night in September, 1712, Pearcival and five other men took control of the fishing smack Lily Ann. The fragile vessel was hardly ideal for carrying out pirate raids, so, before long, Pearcival and his men captured a Spanish barquentine. They used this new ship to hijack the British barque Southwind, twenty days out of Liverpool. Some time later, Pearcival seized a square-rigger, loaded with gold, silver and other treasure.

The members of Pearcival's crew were anxious to head for land and dispose of their ill-gotten cargo, but Pearcival had other ideas. His plan was to share the wealth only with those who had sailed with him on the Lily Ann. After one or two crewmembers disappeared, the rest of the men became suspicious and hatched a plot to overthrow Pearcival. Not long after, a staged scuffle brought Pearcival on deck and crewman John Constance bashed his head in. The ship caught fire, burned to the water and sank, taking most of the crewmen and all the precious cargo to the bottom.

Other pirates also played a part in this horrendous chapter of Newfoundland's history. In 1673, for instance, Dutch privateer Jacob Everson used four armed ships to attack St. John's. Captain Christopher Martin and twenty-three other fishing masters fought off the attack.

Another pirate named Anstis and another named Bartholomew Roberts ravaged the Newfoundland coast in 1721. Roberts attacked and pillaged Trepassey, sinking all but one of the twenty-two ships anchored in the harbour. That same year, shipwright John Phillips came from England to Newfoundland, rounded up some fishermen and set sail for the Caribbean. During an eight-month period, Phillips and his men seized thirty-three ships, but some of their captives eventually overpowered them.

Probably the most dreaded pirates to frequent Newfoundland waters were the Sallee Rovers, so named because they sailed from the port of Sallee in North Africa. Although these pirates came from all corners of the globe, they flew the Turkish flag. Hence the word Turks in reference to pirates.

For sheer brutality and coldbloodedness, few pirtaes can equal the husband and common-law wife team of Eric and Maria Cobham, who sailed from Sandy Point in St. George's Bay, applying their special brand of terror for twenty years. The Cobhams found easy targets in the ships which sailed out of the Gulf of St. Lawrence, often loaded with valuable furs. To cover their bloody tracks, the Cobhams murdered anyone they captured.

Giving up their life of piracy, the Cobhams retired to France, bought a large estate near Le Havre and became members of the nobility. For twelve years, Eric Cobham served as a magistrate and judge in French rural courts. Maria finally drank poison and jumped off a cliff.

Some years later, as he lay dying, Eric Cobham told his horrific life story to a priest, with the stipulation that the confession be published. The priest carried out the request, but the Cobham family bought all copies of the publication and burned them. Nevertheless, one incomplete copy of Cobham's confession survives in the French archives.

Not all the pirates who plundered ships and towns around Newfoundland were of English origin. There was, for example, the French pirate Michel de Sance, who sailed into St. John's in 1596. Unaware of de Sance's less than savoury reputation, Richard Clark and other English captains in St. John's harbour invited the French captain to have breakfast with them. De Sance told them he wasn't feeling well and invited the captains to have breakfast on board his own ship. The unsuspecting men complied and went on board de Sance's ship, where they were held for nine days while de Sance and his men looted their ships. American pirates too left their mark, often stealing food and leaving people to starve, until the British navy put an end to these attacks.

Not everybody hated the pirates, who were known to sell their stolen goods to settlers at bargain prices. Besides, there was a lot more money in piracy than in either fishing or farming. Sir William Vaughan, who lived at Ferryland in the 1620s, estimated that more than 1,500 Newfoundland men had joined pirate crews "to the great hurt of the plantations." As long as piracy thrived and was profitable, there were men willing, even eager, to take risks and satisfy their thirst for adventure and the potential riches that came with it.

L'ANSE-AUX-MEADOWS:
Shades Of The Vikings

Mount Everest, Nepal; the Grand Canyon, U. S. A.; Yellowstone National Park, U. S. A.; Galapagos Islands, Ecuador; the Pyramids, Egypt; L'Anse-aux-Meadows, Newfoundland. Question: What do all these places have in common? Answer: UNESCO (The United Nations Educational, Scientific and Cultural Organization) has declared all of these World Heritage Sites, entitled to special protection. In 1978, L'Anse-aux-Meadows became the first place to receive the UNESCO designation. Today, L'Anse-aux-Meadows, the only authenticated Viking site in North America, is one of four Canadian World Heritage Sites.

Many historians believe L'Anse-aux-Meadows is the place the Vikings called Vinland. And, although you won't find any grapes here, you will find plenty of berries – succulent currants, squashberries, partridgeberries and bakeapples.

The name L'Anse-aux-Meadows probably comes from the French l'anse aux meduses, meaning "bay of jellyfish", for the French settled here back in 1713. But the history of this storied spot goes back much further, to at least five thousand years ago, when Maritime Archaic Indians lived here. Carbon dating also indicates that the Maritime Archaic Indians also lived in these parts as recently as the tenth century, A. D. Dorset Eskimos made this place their home from the sixth to the ninth centuries, A. D.

No doubt most people who have heard of L'Anse-aux-Meadows associate the place with Leif Eiriksson and his fellow seafaring Vikings, who, archaeologists tell us, lived here almost 500 years before Italian explorer Giovanni Caboto sighted the rocky Newfoundland shores. The first Viking to lay his eyes on Vinland was probably Bjarni Herjulfsson, an Icelandic trader swept off course on a voyage to Greenland. Bjarni did not go ashore at Vinland, but he told his story of new lands to the west to other more adventurous characters.

Around 1,000 A. D., Leif Eiriksson (Leif the Lucky) became the first to retrace Bjarni's route. After sailing for about nine days, Leif and his crew stepped ashore at a place they later called Vinland and tasted the sweet dew on the grass. The following spring, Leif and his people sailed back to Greenland with a load of timber and grapes (which could have been berries).

Leif's brother, Thorvald, later led a tragic expedition to Vinland, a voyage which ended in Thorvald's death at the hands of the natives whom they called Skraelings (probably Eskimos). Later still, Thorfinn Karlsefni, a Norwegian sea captain, set out with sixty people, livestock and other supplies, with the intention of setting up a permanent settlement at Vinland. They reached their destination and, late that fall, Karlsefni's wife, Gudrid Torbjornsdottir, gave birth to Snorri, the first white child born in the New World. This attempt at settlement was abandoned too, after repeated skirmishes with the natives.

Freydis, daughter of Eirik the Red, was one of the leaders on the last major expedition to Leif's Vinland colony. This venture also ended in disaster, with Freydis and her followers murdering the other colonists.

When I first visited the L'Anse-aux-Meadows site in the late 1970s, the only visible signs that someone might have lived here were some overgrown mounds rising near the banks of a gentle, meandering brook. Having a passing knowledge of the history of this place, I could imagine stepping back in time to see the Vikings, unshaven, weary and hungry after the long ocean voyage, excitedly dashing ashore and savouring this new, uncharted land, with its trees, grass, game, berries and fish. Here was a place which must have seemed far more inviting and promising than the barren terrain of Greenland.

Some years later, in the early 1980s, I visited L'Anse-aux-Meadows again. This time, there was more to see – exhibits inside the Visitor's Interpretation Centre presented a fascinating account of Norse history and culture, while outside, the United Nations flag flapped impressively in the cool breeze, and eight sod buildings near the original excavations told more of the story. I could imagine a Viking family chatting noisily as they sat around the fire inside their sod hut, a blacksmith forging his nails, using iron from the nearby bog, a Norse fisherman spearing salmon or trout in Black Duck Brook. Then the fog rolled in and the quiet, little town of L'Anse-aux-Meadows assumed an almost mystical character, evocative of a time when there were no fishermen's wharves or neat clapboard houses with lines full of clothes a mere hundred yards away. Now I could all but hear the Vikings sloshing ashore from their shallow, high-prowed boats and running excitedly over the grassy, undulating landscape.

Back in 1913, Newfoundland historian W. A. Munn published a pamphlet in which he wrote: "I believe that when Leif started to come towards the land he was just south of Belle Isle at the break of day, and when he came to land, the island mentioned (in the Viking Sagas) is Sacred Island, just to the north of Cape Onion. They went ashore at Lancey Meadows, as it is called today."

Later, Finnish geographer Vainion Tanner, who worked in Newfoundland from 1937 to 1939, linked the Vikings to the L'Anse-aux-Meadows site. In the early 1950s, New Jersey historian Arlington H. Mallery poked around Pistolet Bay near the tip of the Great Northern Peninsula, but turned up nothing. In 1960, having read Munn's manuscript, Danish archaeologist Jorgen Meldgaard also explored Pistolet Bay, but found nothing to suggest that a Viking settlement had ever existed there.

The next year, local fisherman George Decker directed Norwegian explorer and author Helge Ingstad to a place local people called "The Old Indian Camp", in Sacred Bay, just around the point from Pistolet Bay. Before long, Ingstad was convinced he had struck a golden vein of history and had found the place where the Vikings had lived and laughed and struggled to survive almost a thousand years before. For the next eight years, Helge and his archaeologist wife Anne Stine Ingstad, often braving the tide of skepticism running against them, led groups from Canada, the United States, Scandinavia and Iceland in uncovering and studying more remnants of the Vikings' Vestervegen (Westward) Period. The Ingstads unearthed the remains of several houses – including one eighty-feet long – a sauna, a cooking pit, a charcoal pit and smithy, and shallow depressions suggestive of Norse boatsheds. The excavators also dug up several items almost certainly of Norse origin – a stone lamp, a spindle whorl or spinning stone, a ring-headed bronze pin common to Norse cultures of the ninth and tenth centuries, a bone needle, and iron nails and fragments. In all, some 2,400 items have been recovered from the site.

In 1968, Canada's Minister of Indian Affairs and Northern Development declared the L'Anse-aux-Meadows site one of historic significance. In 1970, Scandinavian and Icelandic scholars formed an international research advisory committee, dedicated to studying and preserving this historic piece of real estate. In order to protect the site from further decay or destruction, workers covered the old walls with new sod, placed new turf over the excavated areas, and controlled Black Duck Brook to prevent flooding of the precious ruins. In 1977, Parks Canada assumed control of L'Anse-aux-Meadows and declared it a National Historic Site. The rest, as we say, is history, with the United Nations adding its considerable weight to the reputation of this site a year later. The area within the park's boundaries now covers close to 20,000 acres, even stretching into the waters of Epaves Bay. In the summer of 1988, a replicated Viking ship, the Gaia, crossed the Atlantic from Iceland and anchored off L'Anse-aux-Meadows, re-enacting a journey and conjuring up visions of almost a thousand years earlier.

If you are fascinated by history or you're just a tourist itching for a taste of something different, a trip to L'Anse-aux-Meadows, at the tip of the Great Northern Peninsula, is well worth the drive. The peaceful brook, the rolling waves caressing the shallow beach, the fog wafting in over the barren, treeless landscape, rock cairns standing out against the sky atop a nearby hill, the excavations, the reconstructed sod huts, the bakeapple bogs nearby, the meditative quiet of this special place, all evoke a sense of timeless history, world-class history.

THE PORTUGUESE:
Adventure In Their Blood

Some years ago, the government of Portugal presented a statue of that country's famed explorer, Gaspar de Corte Real, to the province of Newfoundland. Today, the giant figure towers sixteen feet in the air, looking out on traffic snaking along the Prince Philip Parkway in front of Confederation Building in St. John's.

Corte Real visited Newfoundland twice in the early 1500s, setting the stage for a centuries-old connection between this province and the country of Portugal. Corte Real went back to his home country with several (some reports say as many as sixty) natives from Newfoundland. Whether these natives were Beothuck Indians or Eskimos is not certain. It is interesting to think that, if they were Beothucks, there might still be descendants of that doomed tribe living today.

Sadly, Corte Real and his crew were lost in 1502, when they reportedly reached Cape Chidley at the chilly northern tip of Labrador. Gaspar's brother, Miguel, crossed the Atlantic in search of Gaspar, but he too was lost with all his crew somewhere off the Labrador coast.

The Corte Real brothers reportedly made their trans-Atlantic voyages in tiny caravels of the Order of Christ, in search of the fabled, ever-elusive Northwest Passage.

Some historians claim that the Portuguese visited Labrador (and possibly the island of Newfoundland) before John Cabot stopped off here in 1497. Researchers suggest that Portuguese explorer Diogo de Teive may have sailed west from the Azores in 1452. In *A Wind From the North,* his 1960 biography of Prince Henry the Navigator of Portugal, British navigator Ernle Bradford wrote that: "Portuguese caravels of his (Prince Henry's) time were capable of sailing as far northwest as the Newfoundland banks ... for day after day he (de Teive) kept on standing to the northwest... Then, to his surprise, he suddenly found that the warm, humid air had turned cold ... strong westerly winds now prevailed, and there was a feeling of ice in the air... If we had no

Statue of Corte Real in St. John's Nfld. Dept. of Development

other record of his voyage, we could be sure that Diogo de Teive had sailed right across the Gulf Stream and come out where the cold Newfoundland (Labrador) current whirls down from the north."

In his 1827 book, *A History of the Island of Newfoundland,* Rev. Lewis Amadeus Anspach quoted Dr. Forrester, whom he said "informs us that as early as the year 1500, the (Newfoundland) fishery was carried on by the Portuguese, Biscanes and French, as well as other nations on the Banks of Shallows, and on the coast to the east and south of the island of Newfoundland."

In his *Collection of Voyages,* first published in Venice in 1556, J. B. Ramusio, who had corresponded with John Cabot's son Sebastian, suggested that Gaspar de Corte Real "was the first captain to navigate in that part of the New World which runs toward the North and Northwest, opposite the inhabited regions of Europe." Regardless of which European first laid eyes on Newfoundland, a Portuguese map of 1502 referred to Newfoundland as "Terra del Rey de Portuguall" - Land of the King of Portugal. Apparently, England's King Henry VIII did not protest the Portuguese claim to this part of the world, so it is possible that the Portuguese may have been here before Cabot.

In 1520, King Manuel I of Portugal authorized explorer Alvarez Fagundes to lay claim to any lands he might discover "within the Portuguese sphere of influence." Fagundes gave Portuguese names to many parts of western Newfoundland, but many of these names were later changed by British or French explorers and settlers.

Around the middle of the sixteenth century, the Spaniard Santa Cruz wrote that Labrador got its name "because a husbandman from the Azores gave tidings and information about it to the King of England when he sent Cabot to discover it." (Lavrador is the Portuguese word for farmer or landowner.) A Mercator map of 1569 gave Newfoundland the name "Terra de Bacallaos" (Land of Codfish) and Labrador the name "Terra Corte Realis." Other maps of the time carried similar designations. Portugal continued to claim ownership of Newfoundland until 1580, when Spain annexed Portugal after Henry's death.

Ever since those early days, Portuguese fishermen have been coming to our shores in pursuit of Gadhus callarias, the lowly codfish. According to historians Harvey and Hatton in their 1883 book, *Newfoundland*, in 1578 Portugal had around fifty ships fishing off Newfoundland. It was the codfish, more than anything else, which kept drawing the Portuguese to these shores. For many years, the Portuguese white fleet fished off Newfoundland and was a common sight in St. John's harbour, until modern draggers replaced those famous full-rigged ships.

The codfish is still precious to the people of Portugal, who consume more than 200,000 tons of fish each year to put their country among the leading fish-eating nations of the world. "I sometimes find it hard to believe that Newfoundlanders go to supermarkets where there is such beautiful cod on sale and still prefer to buy steak," Portuguese emissary Melo Cunha told a reporter some years ago. "In Portugal today, codfish is considered to be as much of a treat as steak is here."

On January 1, 1977, the Canadian government officially proclaimed its jurisdiction over a 200-mile offshore fishing zone, a move which affected the traditional fishing practices of foreign nations like Portugal. Traditionally, Portugal hasn't bought much codfish from

Canada, because they could get better prices from Iceland. "Other countries fishing here sell what they catch," said Cunha, "while we need it for our own people. Therefore, I believe we're in a very good position to get along with the Canadians. They need markets and Portugal has no other solution for its shortage than to buy fish."

If you run your finger along the erratic coastline of Newfoundland, you'll touch dozens of place names of Portuguese origin. Take Portugal Cove, for example, which some historians claim was given its name by the great Corte Real himself. Then there's St. Vincent's, named in honour of the patron saint of Portugal. Cape Race reportedly gets its name from Cabo Raso, near the mouth of Portugal's Tagus River. Fermeuse comes from the Portuguese word formosa, which means beautiful. Other examples of the Portuguese influence include: Cape Spear (from esperar, the Portuguese word for hope); Fogo (from fuego, Portuguese for fire), Baccalieu (from bacallaos or codfish); Manuels, Conception Bay.

On May 26, 1955, the Gil Eannes, mother ship of the Portuguese fishing fleet, steamed into St. John's harbour, carrying a statue of Our Lady of Fatima, which today stands inside the Roman Catholic Basilica in St. John's. The entire Portuguese fleet of 5,000 fishermen contributed toward the gift which, according to a dispatch from the Canadian Embassy in Lisbon, was "designed to symbolize the long and happy relations between the people and fishermen of Newfoundland and Portugal." The figure was presented "in deep appreciation of the customary friendly welcome shown to them by the Canadian fishermen and the entire population and authorities of St. John's, during their yearly call at this port for ships' supplies and assistance."

TWILLINGATE:
A Tale of Two Islands

Twillingate. The name rings and ricochets off the tongue. It arouses the curious streak in people from beyond the area, especially those from outside Newfoundland. The best guess for the origin of the name is that Frenchmen fishing in the area named the islands after Toulinguet, a group of islands near Brest, France. Although the French almost certainly gave Twillingate its name, they never did settle in this bastion of British settlement, where distinctly English surnames like Smith, Young, Clarke and Elliott make up most of the telephone listings.

I remember my father telling me of trips he used to make to Twillingate - by fishing skiff in summer, by horse and sleigh in winter. Often the trip was necessary to carry a sick person across the bay to the well-equipped hospital at Twillingate. Although I grew up only a geographic "stone's throw away", as it were, I was in my thirties before I first visited Twillingate. Since then, I have returned several times to learn more about this picturesque spot.

TWILLINGATE

Twillingate consists of two small islands in the middle of Notre Dame Bay, off the northeast coast of Newfoundland. Not far from here, on December 12, 1882, twenty-two schooners were driven out to sea in a hurricane. The islands are home to some half dozen communities – places like Bluff Head Cove, Crow Head, Durrell and Twillingate itself, service and cultural centre of the islands.

The islands which make up Twillingate weren't always as accessible as they are today. Now you can get there after about an hour's drive from Lewisporte over "The Road To The Isles", a network of causeways built since 1962. The first causeway spans Reach Run from Boyd's Cove to Chapel Island. From there you cross Southern Tickle to Southern Island, then take the Curtis Causeway across Dildo Run and Northern Tickle to New World Island. Skirting the northeast flank of New World Island, the highway then skips across Main Tickle to South Twillingate via a causeway completed in 1973. The final link in the chain is a bridge joining South and North Twillingate Islands.

On the way to Twillingate, you pass places with such unusual names as Virgin Arm, Too Good Arm, Whale's Gulch (now called Valley Pond), and Herring Neck, the place where Sir William Coaker started the Fishermen's Protective Union in 1908. At Dildo Run Park you can sweep your eyes out over an expansive collection of islands dotting Notre Dame Bay like pieces on a distorted chessboard.

While the scenic ocean-side drive and colourful communities are part of the magnetic attraction of this Newfoundland archipelago, the history of the area offers its own intrigue. Like many other communities in this province, Twillingate can turn back the clock a few centuries, as Frank and Stanley Curtis discovered while digging an outhouse pit on September 2, 1966. Their shovels turned up spear points and other unusual items, which appeared to have come from some ancient civilization. Ancient indeed. Archaeologists later dated the relics back to around 1,500 B. C. and the Maritime Archaic Indians, who inhabited parts of Newfoundland, Quebec and Maine long before the Vikings stepped ashore near the tip of the Great Northern Peninsula. It was at Twillingate too that Shanawdithit, also known as Nancy, the last of the Beothucks, lived with the family of John Peyton after her capture in 1823.

It seems that fishing families first settled here in the early eighteenth century, although Twillingate had been an important fishing port before that time. In a 1738 census, Captain Vanburgh counted 184 people at

Long Point Lighthouse Calvin Coish

Twillingate, including 152 permanent residents. The community had two ships and six smaller boats. That year, residents salted 12,000 quintals of codfish and produced seal oil worth 440 pounds. Around 1760, the fishermen of Twillingate began to sail north to the rich fishing grounds off Labrador.

In 1812, with the United States at war with England, the Royal Engineers sized up Newfoundland's defences. As a result of their assessment, the engineers recommended that guns be placed at Crow Point and Carter Point, to guard the entrance to Twillingate harbour. At that time, there were 800 people living at Twillingate. By 1857, the population had increased to 2,348 and the town boasted 400 fishing vessels and forty sealing ships. Today, the population of Twillingate Islands is around 4,000.

Like the now-beleaguered codfishery, the annual seal hunt had long been an economic mainstay of Twillingate, indeed the whole of Notre Dame Bay. During the spring of 1862, the residents of Twillingate killed more than 30,000 seals. That was the year the ice jammed close to the shore in early March, loaded with seals. Just about everyone in the community was involved in taking seals when the wind veered and took the ice and seals out to sea. In the storm, four or five men died, including two who drifted off on the ice and were never found. On March 14, the wind swung around to the northeast and pushed the ice tight to the land again. Three days later, the "Great Seal Haul" began in earnest. "The golden and greasy harvest continued for over one month and many men ... made that spring one hundred pounds each," reported Parsons' Christmas Annual of 1900. "One woman whose husband had been ill for several years and (who had) young children took her rope and gaff and, like a true heroine, earned many pounds toward feeding her little ones and added a few comforts to the happiness and the welfare of her suffering husband."

As in most Newfoundland communities, religion has long been a central aspect of life in Twillingate. The town's first Anglican priest was Reverend John Leigh, who came to Twillingate on October 3, 1816. On July 1, 1827, Reverend John Inglis, Lord Bishop of Nova Scotia, consecrated the first St. Peter's Church and Burial Ground and confirmed ninety-three people. The present St. Peter's Church was built in 1842.

In 1831, Methodists of the area, seen as dissenters by the Church of England, began to hold secret meetings. Yet it was not until 1842 that the first Methodist missionary, Reverend William Marshall, arrived at Twillingate. In 1884, Twillingate had 1,109 Anglicans, 2,477 Wesleyans (Methodists), twenty-seven Roman Catholics and seventy-eight Congregationalists. In 1890, Captain Collier brought the Salvation Army to these islands.

The colourful history of Twillingate included the story of a world famous opera singer. Born in 1867, Georgina Stirling studied singing and music in France, Italy and Germany and, in deference to her home town, took the stage name Marie Toulinguet. She toured all over the world, returning every now and then to perform at Twillingate and St. John's in aid of charity. William Temple, editor of the Twillingate Sun, described Miss Toulinguet as " a very striking woman, a woman of strong opinions, but very sociable, very aristocratic."

But not everyone was so kind in describing this plain-looking opera singer from Twillingate. In fact, after hearing her sing, one Italian maestro reportedly told her:

"Ah, mademoiselle, you have the voice of an angel, but the face of the devil." A monument at Snelling's Cove pays tribute to Miss Stirling.

For almost 73 years, beginning in 1880, Twillingate had its own daily newspaper, *The Sun*. The paper carried world, Newfoundland and local news. And advertisements like this one: "Adams' Indian Salve, unequalled for cuts, burns, sores of all kinds, frost bite, dry scurvy of the hands, dry piles and all sores, eruptions, ulcers or diseases for which healing ointments are required. This salve is also excellent for galls on horses. Price: twenty-five cents per box. Sold throughout Newfoundland and may be obtained by wholesale at *The Sun* office, Twillingate."

In the early 1920s, *The Sun* issued an appeal for money to construct a hospital at Twillingate; the appeal raised $20,000. The hospital was opened in 1924 and soon earned a reputation for first-class medical service. The first superintendent of the hospital was Dr. Charles E. Parsons. In 1930, Dr. John M. Olds, a student doctor from Windsor, Connecticutt, came to Twillingate. In 1934, when Dr. Parsons retired, Dr. Olds took over as the hospital's director. For two years during the Second World War, Dr. Olds was the only doctor at Twillingate. In 1968 he was presented with the Centennial Medal; the following year, he was given the Medal of the Order of Canada for his dedicated service to the people of Twillingate and area. Perhaps the most fitting accolade to the doctor, who ranks with the likes of Grenfell in local eyes, is that the high school at Twillingate is now called J. M. Olds Collegiate.

Today, the modern Notre Dame Bay Memorial Hospital stands on the hillside overlooking the harbour of Twillingate. The new brick structure has first-class Xray facilities, nine examination rooms, a physiotherapy department and an excellent library. When it opened, the hospital had a staff of thirty nurses and five doctors.

Some of the fascinating history of this area is on display at the Twillingate museum, which once served as the Anglican Rectory. Here the visitor will see a treadle printing press, a penny farthing bicycle, a hurdy-gurdy, even a ring made from a piece of a German Zeppelin shot down during World War I. Another museum at Durrell depicts life in a Newfoundland fishing community at the turn of this century. At Sleepy Cove, you can take a stroll through Seabreeze Municipal Park, where a copper mining operation flourished in the early 1900s, until it closed in 1920. The Long Point Lighthouse, one of the last manned lighthouses in Newfoundland, continues to be popular with visitors.

Above all, if you come to this part of Newfoundland in the summertime, don't forget your camera. For here, in the middle of July or August, you're likely to see a giant tower of ice grounded just offshore, glinting in the sun. One summer the lighthouse keeper at Long Point counted eighty. And there's much more to see in this fascinating corner of Newfoundland.

RED BAY:
Basking In History

Red Bay. Not a particularly unusual name, although it does contain a little "colour". But Red Bay is an unusual place, offering historians and archaeologists a rare opportunity to study a period of history about which little is known – the time between the voyages of Cartier and Roberval (from 1534 to 1542) and those of Champlain (in the early 1600s).

Fishermen have long considered Red Bay, with its red granite cliffs rising boldly at the water's edge, the best harbour on the coast of southern Labrador. During the Second World War, six corvettes and a mother ship took shelter in this harbour.

Probably the biggest drawing-card at Red Bay is a sunken wreck believed to be that of the 300-ton Spanish whaling galleon San Juan, which sank during a savage storm in 1565. Marine archaeologist Robert Grenier, head of marine excavations for Parks Canada, located the wreck in September of 1978.

For quite some time, historians had known of the Basque presence in North America, but little concrete evidence of that presence had been discovered. That is, until the persistent efforts of Selma Barkham uncovered a virtual gold mine of history. Mrs. Barkham, a determined, meticulous, historical geographer, came upon the Red Bay connection while doing research related to the restoration of Fortress Louisbourg in Nova Scotia. During her investigations, Mrs. Barkham came upon a record of a legal claim which two brothers from the Basque region of northern Spain had launched some four centuries earlier in an attempt to get their fair share of the revenue from the lucrative whale oil retrieved from the sunken San Juan. Little wonder the brothers tried to get a share of the profits, for historians tell us that, back in the 1500s, a barrel of whale oil could fetch fifty times what a barrel of crude oil does these days.

At any rate, in the spring of 1977, Mrs. Barkham took her theory that the Basques had operated a whaling station at Red Bay in the 1500s to archaeologist James Tuck at Memorial University. "Ninety-nine times out of a hundred, something like that turns out to be nothing," said Tuck. "Once in a while it turns out to be something." This particular hunch of Selma Barkham has turned out to be something indeed, as Tuck, Grenier and others have confirmed.

The Basques of Red Bay came from both France and Spain. The French called the busy port Havre de Buttes, while the Spanish used various corruptions of that French name.

While voyages to the New World were popular among Basque fishermen, life wasn't always easy for those who ventured to these shores. Weather and ice conditions weren't always the best, to say nothing of the conflicts between French and Spanish Basques. Back in 1554, during a war between France and Spain, thirteen French

RED BAY

Basque ships captured four Spanish Basque ships and escorted them into Red Bay. Not that battles of this sort were the normal state of relations between French and Spanish Basques. Indeed, the two groups often co-operated, sharing the same ports and teaming up to tow the large whales they killed to shore. Moreover, the wealthier Spanish Basque merchants often served as outfitters for the French Basque ships. One of the biggest problems the Basques had involved clashes with local Eskimos – clashes in which combatants sometimes lost their lives.

Initially, said Barkham, the Basques concentrated on fishing, while killing an occasional whale, salting the meat and taking it back to France for food. Around the late 1530s, the Basques became more involved in killing whales, boiling down the fat to produce oil. Later they used ovens to render down the blubber instead of boiling it.

The larger Basque ships or galleons generally remained in sheltered bays and harbours and served to hold processed whale oil delivered to them by smaller boats called shallops. Barkham estimates that as many as twenty or thirty Basque ships, carrying up to 2,000 men in total, might have crossed the Atlantic to Labrador during a single season. Some of the larger ships of 500 to 750 tons could carry as much as 2,000 barrels of oil. As much as 20,000 barrels of whale oil could have been taken to Europe in a year.

Unlike Basque fishermen who stayed in Labrador only during the summer months, the Basque whalers often stayed until mid-January or so. Researchers speculate that ice, which packs in for hundreds of miles along the Newfoundland coastline during the winter months, may have forced the Basques at times to remain in Labrador even longer than they normally would have.

It isn't surprising then that the whalers constructed more durable buildings than did the transient fishermen. The construction of these more permanent houses helps explain the ubiquitous red roofing tiles still being dug up along the southern coast of Labrador. A 1563 document tells us that the Francisco de Elorriaga was to take "a sufficient quantity of tiles and other materials for the repair of the cabins" on its voyage to the Province of Terranova. In a 1564 report, harpooner Simon de Azcoitia referred to "the cabin they had made for the boiling down of whales they kill."

The whaling industry in southern Labrador seems to have declined after the early part of the seventeenth century, probably because of a shortage of capital following the costly and disastrous (for the Spanish) 1588 Spanish Armada, the loss of the traditional trade route to Belgium, and possibly because of a decreasing whale population as well.

Excavations around Red Bay have uncovered hundreds of valuable artifacts – augers, adzes, a chisel, ceramic jars, bowls, rosary beads, coins, hundreds of barrel staves, a swivel gun, timbers, a huge oak capstan, and other items. Huge quantities of whale bone have been dug up near Red Bay and at other locations.

In 1978, Robert Grenier led a four-man team of divers in exploring the waters around Red Bay. With no great difficulty, the team located the sunken hulk of what historians believe is the San Juan. Much work has been carried out at Red Bay in the years since. Some items from the San Juan are on display at the National Archives in Ottawa, but most of the ship's remains have been carefully put back into the silt on the ocean floor, where they had been well preserved for more than four hundred years.

Each segment of the San Juan has been closely studied, and there are plans to build a model one-tenth the size of the San Juan, using shipbuilding techniques employed by the Basques during the sixteenth century. Robert Grenier has said that the wreck provided priceless information concerning the evolution of shipbuilding during the European Renaissance.

Mrs. Barkham has also discovered numerous other documents relating to Basque settlement in Labrador. Documents such as insurance policies, a 1547 agreement with coopers (barrelmakers) around Blanc Sablon, cargo charters, and what are probably the oldest existing wills written in North America (in 1577 and 1584). In 1974, Mrs. Barkham became the Canadian National Archives' official representative in Spain.

The Royal Canadian Geographical Society gave Selma Barkham and her colleagues financial assistance to carry out research into the history of the Basques in Newfoundland. The Social Sciences and Humanities Research Council came up with funds for the publication of Mrs. Barkham's findings. Late in 1978, the Newfoundland government announced they were declaring Red Bay a Provincial Historic Site.

In 1980 the Royal Canadian Geographical Society presented Selma Barkham with their gold medal, in recognition of her "splendid dedication and singlemindedness". It was indeed a well-deserved chance for Mrs. Barkham to "bask" in the glory of her outstanding contribution to our knowledge of the past.

In the summer of 1983, archaeologists like Dr. Tuck and his assistants unearthed some fifty skeletons buried near Red Bay. That same summer, workers also discovered another sunken Basque wreck similar to the San

DISTANT SHORES

Juan. This would suggest that the full story of Red Bay's colourful past has not yet been told.

Archaeological dig at Red Bay Nfld. Dept. of Development

BRIGUS:
A Glorious Past

Exactly where the name Brigus came from is a matter of some debate. French priest Abbe Baudoin, who came to Newfoundland with d'Iberville's forces in the late 1600s, suggested it might have come from the French word "brigue", which means canvassing. Newfoundland historian M. F. Howley believed the name to be a corruption of Brig Harbour. The most likely explanation is that the town is named after Brighouse (pronounced Brigus), a community in Huddersfield, Yorkshire. No matter what its origin, the name Brigus can summon visions of rough and ready ships and men setting out for the seal hunt and fully-rigged schooners with their hardy crews heading north to the Labrador summer fishery.

Local tradition holds that the Spracklins purchased the half of Brigus which extends from Battery Brook to the drawbridge from John Guy, who founded the nearby community of Cupids around 1610. A 1675 census gave the population of Brigus as thirty-four. In 1697, Abbe Baudoin wrote in his journal that Brigus was "a well established English settlement, where there were about sixty men." Baudoin estimated that the eleven crews fishing out of Brigus caught some 6,000 quintals of fish that year.

Like many Newfoundland communities, Brigus came under attack from French forces. In the late 1690s, the settlers at Brigus surrendered to d'Iberville and his men, who had already taken several settlements in Conception Bay. French forces pillaged the town again in 1705. Despite such attacks, the community not only survived, but prospered.

The town of Brigus had an influx of settlers from the British Isles - Cozens, Leamons, Gushues, Perceys, Normans, Mundens. You can still find these names, or variations of them, in the Brigus section of the telephone directory. One part of the community was traditionally called Englishtown, another Irishtown, and there is spec-

Brigus Nfld. Dept. of Development

ulation there may have been a Jerseytown, since many of the early inhabitants, such as the Normans, came from Jersey.

Brigus' connection with the seal hunt goes back at least a couple of centuries. In 1778, for example, sealer William Munden landed 10,000 seal pelts at Brigus. Sealing historian L. G. Chafe offered an explanation for the town's prominence in the sealing industry. Chafe wrote that "The situation of the harbour, with wide mouth, its high lands and deep water right to the cliff gave the ice no chance to hold on when the westerly wind blew and therefore the craft found their way out much more easily than from other harbours in the bay." In 1857, thirty-eight sealing ships sailed from Brigus. In 1868, the number was down to twenty-seven and the community's reputation as the sealing capital of Newfoundland was fading. In 1872, only fifteen ships headed out from Brigus in search of seals. One intriguing holdover from Brigus' sealing heyday is a 100-foot-long tunnel which Cornish miner John Hoskins blasted through the solid cliff in 1883 to give the seafaring Bartletts access to the crowded harbour.

If any name is synonymous with the port of Brigus, that name is Bartlett. The most famous was Captain Bob Bartlett who, in 1908, sailed into the history books as captain of the Roosevelt, the ship which took Admiral Robert Peary to a spot just over 450 miles from the North Pole. Bartlett later took part in twenty other Arctic expeditions, including those of Vilhjalmur Stefansson. In 1917, Bartlett rescued Commander MacMillan's stranded expedition, which had gone in search of the illusory Crocker Land. In 1926, as captain of the Effie M. Morrissey, Bartlett took George Palmer Putnam, publisher, explorer and husband of aviation pioneer Amelia Earhart, on an American Museum expedition to North Greenland. Danish explorer Rasmussen called Bob Bartlett "the world's greatest ice captain."

In 1928, Bartlett published his memoirs under the unassuming title *The Log of Bob Bartlett*. In the book, Bartlett related how, each spring, anywhere from 1,000 to 1,500 men, some of them having trudged a hundred miles or more, would converge on the tiny community of Brigus, eagerly jostling for the "privilege" of purchasing a berth on a sealing vessel.

During February, the crews would be busy hauling firewood and logs for building ship spars and small boats called punts. On the first of March, the ships would sail out of Brigus. As Bartlett recalled, some years the harbour at Brigus was frozen solid. When that happened, the crews of some forty to sixty ships would all pitch in and saw a channel through the ice to the open sea. For ten days or more the men would work like horses, singing rousing chanties to keep up the momentum as well as their spirits. Eventually, a channel cleared, the ships would push into it one by one to form a forest of masts and billowing sails headed for the ocean and, eventually, the ice floes. As Bartlett wrote simply, "it made a great sight."

In recognition of his involvement in Polar exploration, Captain Bob Bartlett received several awards, including the Kane Medal of the Geographical Society of Philadelphia, the Charles P. Daly Medal of the American Geographical Society, and the United States Congressional Peary Polar Expedition Medal. Captain Bob also joined a very select group - Admiral Peary, Roald Amundsen, Dr. Grove Clark Gilbert, Sir Ernest Shackleton, Richard Byrd, and Charles Lindbergh - when the National Geographic Society gave him its Hubbard

Medal.

In 1981, Memorial University officially named its Centre for Cold Ocean Resources Engineering (C-CORE) in St. John's the Robert A. Bartlett Building. Hawthorne Cottage, built by Captain Bob's maternal grandfather in 1800, was moved six miles from its original site and now stands in the centre of Brigus as a memorial to the legacy of Bob Bartlett. In 1982, Judge Rupert Bartlett, owner of the house and a nephew of the famous captain, unveiled a plaque on behalf of the Canadian government to declare the distinctive one-and-a-half storey house a National Historic Site.

Captain Bob Bartlett's father, William James, and his grandfather Abram were both renowned mariners. Captain Abram Bartlett skippered a sealing ship, the Panther, for seventeen years and landed a total of 143,473 pelts. For quite a few summers, Captain Abram also sailed the Panther to Turnavik, Labrador, where he managed a prosperous fishing enterprise. Captain William James Bartlett took part in the seal hunt and the Labrador fishery for forty-two years. He set a record total catch of 444,801 seals for the Gulf of St. Lawrence, and served as mate on Dr. Isaac Hayes' 1869 expedition to the North Pole.

The Bartlett clan also produced other prominent mariners, including Captain Henry B. Bartlett, who commanded the Falcon during Peary's 1893 expedition to northern Greenland. Captain John Bartlett also commanded ships on several of Peary's voyages and later served in the Newfoundland House of Assembly. He earned the nickname "Honest John", because of his election campaign, during which he called for a public grindstone for every community in his district of Port de Grave, so that "every man could grind his own axe at the public's expense."

Captain Moses Bartlett took part in Peary's 1905-1906 expedition and commanded the Bradley on Dr. Frederick Cook's voyage to the Arctic. Captain Samuel W. Bartlett, an uncle of Captain Bob, captained the Neptune to the Arctic in 1903 to help set up a customs and justice network in Canada's north. Captain William "Follow On" Bartlett, earned a reputation for his persistence and daring in searching for the seal herds. Captain Isaac Bartlett rescued Captain Tyson and his crew, who had drifted 1,500 miles on an iceberg.

When the town of Brigus was incorporated in 1964, Frederick Bartlett became the first mayor.

Another Brigus captain, William Norman, went to Bedford Pim Island in 1884 in the Polaris to rescue the seven survivors of Admiral Adolphus Washington Greely's ill-fated Arctic expedition.

The people of Brigus also tell stories about another one-time resident, American artist Rockwell Kent, who lived in the community in the early part of this century. Kent left Newfoundland amid rumours that he was a German spy. Back in the United States, he was accused of being a Communist sympathizer. Later, in an effort to make amends for their unfounded suspicions, the Newfoundland government brought Kent back to Newfoundland and put on a sumptuous dinner in his honour.

The steady decline in the number of ships taking part in the annual seal hunt coincided with a decrease in the population of Brigus. By 1891, the population of the little port had fallen to 1,541 from its high of 2,365 during the middle of the nineteenth century. By 1901, the population of Brigus was down to 1,162; by 1945 it had fallen below 900. Today, just over a thousand people call this classic Newfoundland outport their home.

Brigus Harbour Nfld. Dept. of Development

THE EATON'S CATALOGUE:
A Newfoundland Tradition

I remember it well. It was one of my favourite Christmas gifts – a shiny, silver-grey helicopter outfitted with batteries and "remote" control. With practice, I learned to keep it gliding more or less gracefully around the room for a couple of minutes.

Thinking back to that memory of a childhood Christmas, I am reminded of something else which was for many years a vital part of Christmas in Newfoundland, indeed, all of Canada. I'm referring to the Eaton's Catalogue, which came to rank with janneying and the Doyle News as honoured traditions in this corner of the nation.

January 14, 1976 was a sad day for many Newfoundlanders. That was the day Eaton's announced it was closing its mailorder department and getting rid of its famous catalogue, including the eagerly-awaited Christmas edition.

For us, telephone orders were out of the question for the simple reason that, for many years, the only phone in our community was the old wooden crank-style one at the post office run by my grandmother. Even when Bell's marvelous invention became more commonplace, long-distance calls weighed heavily on the pocket books of austere fishermen.

The ritual began as young and old collected themselves around the oilcloth-draped kitchen table to chat about the latest colours and styles. There they would pore avidly over the colourful pages and, if budgets allowed, fill out one of the neatly-lined order forms headed with the words "The T. Eaton Company". The order could be for almost anything – a new hat, kid gloves, pile-lined parkas, longjohns, even a gasoline-powered washing machine. In preparation for Christmas, and to keep the youngsters happy, there might be a few toys on the order, too.

When snow blanketed the ground and ice jammed the harbour and covered the ponds, we would anxiously await the familiar drone of the little, red and white, single-engine Beaver. If the ice was thick enough, the landing area would be lined with boughs to guide the pilot. Otherwise, the plane would be forced to abort its landing and head back to its home base at Gander, disappointing many eager customers.

After swinging a couple of circles around the community to announce its arrival, the peppy flying machine would touch down deftly and skim along a hundred yards or so on the ice. When the plane could land, there would be a few canvas bags of mail, which the mailman (who happened to be my father) and his trusty horse would haul to the post office. Among the mail there would usually be a sizable pile of C.O.D. parcels, many from Eaton's. It was a rare Newfoundland youngster indeed who didn't know the meaning of the initials

C.O.D. long before he was old enough to don corduroy trousers and knee rubbers.

Around Christmastime, a familiar sound was the jingle of bells and the heavy scuff of hooves as horses with sleighs in tow pulled up in front of the post office. From each sled, a rider would dismount, then rush into the office, emerging with a parcel or two, sometimes an armful. A perfunctory "giddup" and another satisfied Eaton's customer would disappear over the hill.

The story of Eaton's goes back to 1869, when Timothy Eaton gave up his share in a small dry goods store his brother and he were running near London, Ontario. Later, Timothy moved to Toronto and went into business on his own. His company prospered and established a solid reputation, touting the guarantee of "Goods satisfactory or money refunded." In twenty years, the T. Eaton Company became well known all across Canada and in Newfoundland, which had not yet joined Confederation.

In 1884, the company brought out its first simple catalogue, a thirty-two page price list without illustrations. Before long, the growing enterprise was putting out two catalogues per year – Spring/Summer and Fall/Winter issues. In addition, they produced a variety of specialty catalogues for drugs, groceries, seeds, and building and farm supplies. There were even special bicycle catalogues, offering bicycles for $100 to $150 each, quite a sum in those days.

More than anything else, it was the Christmas edition of the Eaton's catalogue which heralded the festive season in thousands of Newfoundland homes. The company brought out its first Christmas catalogue in 1894. Today, copies of the first two editions are extremely hard to come by; even the Eaton's archives doesn't have them.

The sixteen-page Christmas volume of 1896 carried the slogan: "T. Eaton Company - Canada's Greatest Store". The 1897 catalogue ran to seventy-five pages and the company was now billing itself as "The Headquarters for Christmas Goods". That year, for the first time, old Saint Nick himself showed up on the back cover. Inside, a thirty-five pound pail of Christmas candy was advertised for three dollars and fifty cents.

In 1901, the famous Eaton Beauty Doll took the Christmas market much as the Cabbage Patch Dolls did some years ago. To own an Eaton's Beauty Doll was the dream of more than a few Newfoundland girls and the dream could be fulfilled for a dollar. With curly hair, china head, and eyes that opened and closed, the doll was promoted as "the best value offered in Canada for the money." In 1942, the doll finally faded from the market, although she still cost only a dollar ninety-nine. In the 1960s, Eaton's put the doll back on the market again, but her popularity had waned and she disappeared again.

Games were all the rage in 1902, and Eaton's was in on the action. "With the long winter evenings comes the increasing demand for indoor games," their catalogue observed. "Recognizing this fact, we have left no stone unturned in our efforts to secure the largest and most varied assortment available and we believe we have been successful. Scores of games for both young and old are to be found in our game section and at prices to suit all purses."

In 1908, for reasons unknown (but probably in an effort to save money), the Eaton's Christmas Catalogue didn't arrive at homes across Canada and Newfoundland. There would not be another edition of the popular publication until 1953. During the forty-five-year interval, shoppers could find a list of Christmas gift suggestions in the Fall/Winter edition.

The Great Depression took its toll on the fortunes of Eaton's and the company was especially careful not to encourage extravagance. To do their bit for the floundering economy, Eaton's included in their catalogues lists of items people on relief could get with their monthly vouchers.

After the Second World War, the profits of Timothy Eaton's company soared once again. When the Christmas catalogue finally re-emerged in 1953, the thirty-five pound pails of candy were gone. But there were smaller tins and a four-pound box of bonbons sold for two seventy-nine. And there was Punkinhead, the little bear that had first appeared in the Eaton's Santa Claus Parade of 1948.

Apart from its obvious virtue as a shopping convenience, the Eaton's catalogue also served a variety of other practical purposes. For example, it was an almost inexhaustible supply of material for the outhouse. An unforgettable teacher I once had, noted for his delightful digressions from the topic under discussion, once recalled a familiar scene from his youth in a Newfoundland outport. The scene was of a Newfoundlander clad snugly in fur-lined parka and leather logans (both probably purchased through the Eaton's catalogue) trudging through knee-deep snowdrifts with a shovel under one arm and a dog-eared Eaton's catalogue tucked under the other.

As children growing up in a small Newfoundland community, we had access to very few books, except for a few school texts. Books were a luxury for the monied business class. For us, the Eaton's catalogue was a kind of substitute for Archie comics and dime novels. For hours, we'd stretch out on the rug in front of the old Regal stove as birch junks snapped briskly in the fire, snipping out pictures of fire engines, boots, faces or whatever caught our fancy.

On February 14, after our limited supply of store-bought valentines had been used up, we'd cut page after page of the catalogue into hundreds of mis-shaped hearts and dump them in through our neighbours' doors. It was a kind of local prank to see who could throw the most valentines in anybody's porch. Anonymously, of course.

It's been reported that some poor illiterates would clip out pictures of items they wished to order and send them to Eaton's. There's the story of one old lady who must have figured she could order anything she saw in the catalogue. It seems that one day she cut out a picture of the most handsome man she could find and sent for him. We don't know if the man ever arrived at the old lady's door, but, given the excellent reputation of Eaton's mail-order service, it would be surprising if they didn't at least try to fill the order.

In its later years, the Eaton's catalogue, even the Christmas edition, lost much of its earlier charm and popularity, largely because of the increased access to shopping malls. In an attempt to recapture some of the old appeal, Eaton's began calling its Christmas catalogue "The Wish Book". Ironically, Canadian Indians had called it exactly that many years earlier. In western Canada, the catalogue had been nicknamed "The Farmer's Bible". Many Newfoundlanders called it "The Women's Bible."

In his novel, *The Swing in the Garden*, Hugh Hood wrote that "the true epic of Canadian life might be told in the story of ... the Eaton's catalogue."

"By 1905," wrote historian Michael Bliss, "one of the few things most Canadians had in common was the fact that they all shopped at Eaton's." For the people of Newfoundland, the Eaton's catalogue was, for many years, the only way to shop.

These days, only Sears carries on the mail-order tradition on a grand scale in Canada. Being something of a nostalgia buff, I've made a point of holding on to that last 1976 edition of the Eaton's catalogue. Who knows? Like those rare earlier editions, it too may one day be a collector's item.

TRINITY:
Living History

We love the place, O God.
Wherein Thine honour dwells,
The joy of Thine abode,
All earthly joy excels.

Many of us know that verse as part of a favourite old hymn. We may even have noticed the author's name in small print at the end - William J. Bullock. But that's about all we know. Where, for example, was the hymn written?

Well, the hymn cited above was composed by Reverend Bullock while he served as clergyman at Trinity, a tiny outport tucked away beside steep cliffs in Trinity Bay. (There's another Trinity in Bonavista Bay, a cozy little community where I began my teaching career.) Bullock's hymn was sung for the first time in 1827, by his Church of England congregation at Trinity.

For twenty years, Bullock was the minister for Trinity and nearby settlements. Bullock later moved to Nova Scotia, where he died in 1874. Some years later, when a new church was constructed at Trinity, Reverend

Bullock's son came from Nova Scotia to take part in the official opening, and the congregation again sang the stirring strains of William Bullock's hymn.

That little story is but a slim chapter in the long, exciting history of one of this country's oldest settlements. Records indicate that Trinity's first settlers sailed from Plymouth, England, aboard the brigantine Hawke in 1558 and landed at the sheltered harbour on June 3. The forty-three people brought with them pigs, sheep, chickens and a generous supply of food.

In the 1800s, Trinity had a sizable population of around 4,000 and was a thriving fishing and shipbuilding community. Today, less than a third that early number live here, but a few more move in all the time. From 1810 to 1860, Trinity was the home of three pros-

Trinity, Trinity Bay Calvin Coish

perous businesses – Slade's, Garland's and Brooking's. The Slade operation alone employed 300 people. There were fifty spots in the town where a thirsty man could quaff a mug of rum for a nickel; today, there are a couple in the area, and the cost is far more than a nickel.

Trinity was the site of a number of notable firsts, including the first smallpox vaccination in North America. The smallpox vaccine was developed by Dr. Edward Jenner of England in the late 1700s. It so happened that Jenner had been a school chum of Rev. John Clinch, a surgeon and clergyman who spent thirty-five years in the village of Trinity and, was, incidentally, Rev. William Bullock's father-in-law. To protect the residents of Trinity against the dreaded smallpox, Clinch obtained some cowpox vaccine from Jenner and administered it to his charges. The last case of smallpox on earth was reported in the late 1970s, and it's interesting to think that a doctor in Newfoundland helped keep the illness in check so many years ago.

John Clinch was born in England and came to Newfoundland in the 1770s, originally settling at Bonavista. In 1775, Reverend Balfour of the Society for the Propagation of the Gospel moved from Trinity to Harbour Grace, leaving Trinity's forty-member Church of England congregation with a new church but no minister. In 1784, 109 Protestants from the Trinity area sent a petition to SPG headquarters in England, requesting that the highly-respected Doctor Clinch be appointed to their community. Impressed by Clinch's credentials, the SPG brought him back to England to be ordained.

In 1786, Clinch took on the huge task of rebuilding the Church, both physically and spiritually; the church building was falling down and there were only eight loyal churchgoers to be found. By 1790, there were a dozen parishioners and the old church had been renovated, as Clinch observed in his report, "not without much pecuniary sacrifice on the part of the minister."

In 1793, Clinch reported that, in the different settlements around Trinity, he had baptized twenty-four adults and fifty-three children. "A spirit of Christianity prevails and in most places I found a well-disposed person who, in every Lord's Day, read the morning and evening service to the Church of England inhabitants at his own or some neighbour's house."

In 1809, Clinch reported thirty Church of England communicants, with growing competition from the Methodists. He lamented the fact that some people were even calling themselves "Church of England Methodists," an obvious contradiction to a loyal Church of Englander like him. Clinch died in 1819 at the age of 72.

Trinity was also the site of North America's first court of justice, constructed in 1615, after the British Admiralty had ordered Sir Richard Whitbourne to do something about the growing crime rate among European fishermen stationed in Newfoundland. It seems this wasn't Whitbourne's first visit to Trinity, as reports suggest that he went there in 1579 to pick up poultry and fish. Whitbourne was also given responsibility for bringing law and order to other parts of the island of Newfoundland. Sir Richard later wrote of Newfoundland's "famous, fair, and profitable rivers ... delightful, large and inestimable woods and ... fruitful and enticing hills and delightful valleys." King James of England was so impressed by Whitbourne's book that he ordered that a copy be sent to every parish in his kingdom.

A rather ironic and fascinating aside to Whitbourne's

time in Newfoundland is that, for eleven days in 1615, the Governor was held captive by the infamous pirate, Peter Easton, who plundered numerous ships and towns along the coast of this island. It seems that Whitbourne came through his hostage incident unharmed.

As suggested earlier, Trinity's growth and prosperity were based mainly on the fishing and shipbuilding industries, which today are closer to memories than anything substantial. This sheltered harbour, with a staggering twenty-one miles of coastline, is one of the best in the world and once attracted ships from all over.

This meant, of course, that Trinity had its own system of impressive defences against attack. The early settlers at Trinity built their first fortifications in 1599 on Admiral's Island. More extensive fortifications, constructed later at what is now called Fort Point, were levelled by the French when they tried to take the town in 1762. Just how successful the French were in their conquest is not clear, but some reports suggest that the settlers, led by such prominent figures as businessman Benjamin Lester, kept the aggressors at bay.

Benjamin Lester lived at Trinity from 1750 until 1768, when he went back home to Poole, England. The Lesters were in the business of making casks for holding fish and shipped fish and oil to England from Newfoundland. One of Lester's daughters married another Poole merchant, George Garland. In 1821, George's sons, George and John Bingley, came to live at Trinity and expanded Lester's original brick house to three and a half storeys. The Ryan brothers, another group of businessmen, bought the house in 1902 and lived there until 1925.

In 1978, the Canadian and Newfoundland governments began a five-year program to restore Trinity to a shade of its former glory. Much of the credit for the restoration of the Garland premises and other historic sites at Trinity must go to the Trinity Historical Society, which spent fifteen years researching the history of the community and pleading with various governments to get things moving.

Evidence of Trinity's rich history isn't restricted to what you can see on dry land. There's almost certainly just as much to see under the salt water in the harbour and bay. For example, during one month in the summer of 1978, the Newfoundland Marine Archaeology Society salvaged 416 artifacts from a wreck believed to be the Speedwell, sunk by ice in 1781. The items recovered included buttons, shoes, bottles, cutlery and wooden carpenter's tools.

Trinity is bursting with history, just begging to be preserved and retold, which is exactly what a theatre troupe did in the summer of 1993, as they staged stories from Trinity's past for the benefit of residents and visitors. There's the old courthouse (although not the one of Whitbourne's day), St. Paul's Anglican Church with the grave of Reverend Doctor Clinch nearby, a restored house crammed with everything from guns to beds to school desks. It's nice to see that all this stuff isn't stowed away in some dingy warehouse or, as we've seen too many times, taken to the nearest dump or sold to mainlanders as "antiques."

FOGO ISLAND:
Still Lots Of Fire

There are still quite a few places in Newfoundland where a person can sit back and enjoy a quiet, relaxing holiday, undisturbed by the whir of traffic and the hectic pace of city living. But nowhere is this slower pace more noticeable than on Fogo Island, a largely untouched slice of the real Newfoundland on the outer reaches of Notre Dame Bay. To get to the island, you take the ferry from Cape Farewell on the island of Newfoundland to Man o' War Cove, near Stag Harbour, on Fogo Island.

There are those who think that the name Fogo originated with the ubiquitous Newfoundland fog, but the name almost certainly has no connection to that particular feature of our volatile weather. The most plausible explanation is that the name comes from the Portuguese word fuego, meaning fire. The fires seen here by early explorers could have been forest fires or the flames of Beothuck Indian encampments. Some early maps referred to the island as Aves or Bird Island.

In spite of organized efforts by a former government

to relocate people living in remote areas of the province, many Fogo Islanders resisted pressure to move. And the island and its people have survived, bolstered by their co-operative determination to make a living here.

Portuguese fishermen and explorers were probably the first Europeans to see Fogo Island. French explorer Jacques Cartier reportedly dropped anchor near the island in 1534. Fogo Island is one of the oldest settled parts of Newfoundland and had inhabitants as early as 1680, many of them taking refuge here after skirmishes with the Beothucks. Others came in pursuit of King Cod. By 1783, there were 215 settlers on Fogo Island. Eventually, some fifteen communities grew up around the island; more than 4,000 people still call this island their home.

Today, the people and communities of Fogo Island present an intriguing microcosm of the traditional Newfoundland way of life, although that way of life is slowly changing even here. At one end the island is barren and treeless; at the other, heavily forested and sheltered. In one community, you'll find mostly Protestants; a few miles away, mostly Roman Catholics. In one community, you'll find a decidedly Newfoundland dialect; in another a heavy Irish brogue.

The unofficial capital of the island is Fogo, a collection of houses and other buildings clustered around a couple of spacious coves at the bleak, rocky, north-western corner of the island. In 1738, the twenty-one families living at Fogo produced 19,000 quintals of fish, two hundred and twenty dollars worth of seal oil, and five hundred dollars worth of furs. In 1981, the town had a population of just over 1,100 people.

Barr'd Islands (several small islands linked by a series of small causeways), is Fogo Island's second-oldest community. Nearby is the curiously-named town of Joe Batt's Arm. Historical records indicate that the English adventurer Captain James Cook, who explored Newfoundland's northeast coast during the 1760s, had a crew member named Joe Batt. For reasons unknown today, Batt left Cook's ship at Gander Bay in 1763. Two years later, he settled on Fogo Island, where he left his now-famous name. Earlier in this century, there was a move to change the name of Joe Batt's Arm to Queenstown, in honour of Queen Victoria, but people objected, so the original name stuck. There's another interesting little story told about the name Joe Batt's Arm. Quite a few years back, this ad appeared in a Newfoundland newspaper: "Wanted: A nurse for Joe Batt's Arm." The British humour magazine Punch got wind of the ad and printed it as an amusing double entendre.

About six miles east of Joe Batt's Arm is the village of Tilting, the end of the road on the northeast side of the island. This community reportedly owes its name to the huts or tilts which served as homes for the earliest settlers. The residents of this Roman Catholic community speak with a distinctive dialect, quite similar to that spoken on the Emerald Isle on the other side of the Atlantic. At one time, it was reported that Tilting had a higher proportion of elderly people than any other Canadian village.

On the other side of Joe Batt's Arm from Tilting is Shoal Bay, the only settlement on the island which did not rely on the fishery for its existence. In 1968, the Fogo Island Co-op obtained money from the Newfoundland government to construct a shipyard at Shoal Bay for building longliners. After producing some thirty vessels, the shipyard ran into financial trouble, then shut down in 1974.

On the southern rim of the island is the community of Seldom-Come-By, generally shortened to Seldom. This name derives from a bygone era, when fishing schooners on the way to and from Labrador seldom passed by, often anchoring in the sheltered harbour overnight. Three miles to the west is the community of Little Seldom.

Stag Harbour is a sheltered little community, surrounded by wooded hills near the southwestern corner of the island, just a few miles from Seldom. The first settlers at Stag Harbour moved here in the 1920s from the neighbouring Indian Islands, now deserted, to avoid the savage storms which often destroyed wharves and fishing gear on the low-lying, sea-swept islands.

About four miles from Stag Harbour as the crow flies is the community of Island Harbour, encircled with fir and spruce and with a small island guarding its entrance. Many of the people here are, like the people of Tilting, of Irish descent. If you sidetrack a little on the road to Island Harbour, you come upon the tiny community of Deep Bay, last town on Fogo Island to get a highway link to the rest of the island.

Besides the communities which still survive, a number of deserted settlements scattered around the island betray hints of life in times past – places like Lion's Den near Fogo; Sandy Cove, near Tilting; Black Head Cove off the Island Harbour Road; Wild Cove near Seldom; Cape Fogo on the island's southeastern corner. These places and others are all deserted now, the abandoned houses taken over by cats, rats and nesting birds, tall grass and trees slowly reclaiming the landscape.

For several summers, the town of Fogo has been staging its Brimstone Head Folk Festival, a celebration of what makes this province unique. If you enjoy a fairly rustic lifestyle or just want a glimpse of what much of Newfoundland used to be like, you'll find what you're looking for here. And nowhere are you more likely to encounter the legendary Newfoundland hospitality than on this piece of granite anchored off the province's northeast coast.

Ferry at Man o' War Cove, Fogo Island   Calvin Coish

HARBOUR GRACE:
Pirate's Hangout

The name is by no means outstanding or unusual in the colourful nomenclature of Newfoundland. Historians suggest that the name Harbour Grace is a mutation of Havre de Grace, now called Le Havre, at the mouth of the River Seine in France. The history of Harbour Grace, a seaport on the western side of Conception Bay, has been anything but ordinary.

Records show that the community of Harbour Grace was probably settled around the middle of the sixteenth century. One of the most notable aspects of the town's early history is that it was the headquarters of pirate Peter Easton, who recruited many Newfoundland fishermen to help him plunder ships anywhere in the Atlantic between Labrador and the Caribbean. Easton is still something of a folk hero in these parts and the pirate's black ensign still flutters outside the Conception Bay Museum. After making a fortune in the waters off North America, Easton went back to France, where he lived in opulence as the Marquis of Savoy.

According to the journal of Pere Beaudoin, in 1670

Harbour Grace had a population of 100 people. French forces led by d'Iberville sacked the town in 1697. The French attacked Harbour Grace again in 1705, causing extensive damage.

In 1771, a Methodist preacher, John Stretton, built a chapel here. That same year, a Church of England clergyman, Reverend Balfour, opened a school under the direction of W. Lampen. Balfour's records put the population of Harbour Grace in 1778 at 5,768. In 1880 the population topped 7,000, but it declined after that. By 1900, a number of factors, including the declining economic fortunes of the area, caused the population of Harbour Grace to drop back to 5,000. By 1940, only 2,000 people lived at Harbour Grace. After Confederation in 1949, the fortunes of this community again picked up. Today, Harbour Grace has a population of around 3,000.

Plaques in the town of Harbour Grace pay tribute to Reverend Lawrence Coughlan, who set up North America's first Wesleyan mission here in 1765, and Sir Thomas Roddick, who was Deputy Surgeon-General in the force that quashed the Northwest Rebellion in 1885 and became Dean of Medicine at McGill University. Reverend Lewis Amadeus Anspach, one of Newfoundland's first historians, lived at Harbour Grace after 1802. Prime Minister Sir Richard Squires was born here, as was the province's second premier, Frank Moores.

Much of the history of Harbour Grace has been wiped out by fires or renovations, but parts of this community still show marks of an earlier vintage. The museum, the courthouse (a national historic site), St. Paul's, the oldest stone church in Newfoundland, and an old stone house, once the office of a thriving business, still stand as reminders of the past.

DISTANT SHORES

The Conception Bay Museum is a nineteenth-century building of brick and stone, a former customs house where Easton's fort used to be. Inside the museum, an exhibit chronicles the history of trans-Atlantic flight, while outside a plaque notes the prominent part this community played in early aviation history.

The first aircraft runway on the island of Newfoundland was built at Harbour Grace. On June 25, 1930, Captain C. Kingsford-Smith and his crew landed the Southern Cross at Harbour Grace, on the last leg of their round-the-world trip which had started on Long Island, New York on May 3.

On July 1, 1931, two American airmen, Wiley Post and Harold Gatty, completed a global flight in eight days

The Kyle near Harbour Grace   Bill Bowman

and fourteen hours. On June 23, they had stopped at Harbour Grace, before going on to Chester, England.

In May, 1932, Amelia Earhart landed at Harbour Grace in her Lockheed Vega Monoplane. She took off from Harbour Grace at 2 p.m. that day and landed at Londonderry, Ireland the following day, going into the history books as the first woman to fly solo across the Atlantic. Between 1926 and 1936, some twenty pioneering flights took off from the runway at Harbour Grace.

But, not all moments in the history of Harbour Grace have been as bright as those aviation glory days. Like in 1861, when an angry mob of 200 people attacked an election candidate. Prime Minister Hoyles promptly took away the district's election privileges. Six months later, during preparations for a by-election, a constable was killed. The Harbour Grace seat remained vacant for some time after that.

Another incident, which happened in 1883, became known as the Harbour Grace Affray. It was December 26 and 400 Orangemen were parading through the Roman Catholic section of the community. The ruckus between Protestants and Catholics which followed left at least five men dead.

That same year, an earth tremor shook an island off the mouth of Harbour Grace, literally splitting it in two. The lighthouse, along with the keeper and his family, were left stranded near the edge of the divide. Not surprisingly, the keeper resigned his job and an automatic beacon went into service there.

For many years, Harbour Grace was a major commercial centre for the surrounding area. One of the largest businesses at Harbour Grace was started by Scotland native John Munn, who came to Newfoundland in 1825. Munn worked for eight years with Baine Johnston and

Company in St. John's. In 1833, Munn moved to Harbour Grace and opened a business with William Punton, another Scotsman. After 1872, the business operated under the name of John Munn and Company. Munn built his firm into what came to be called "the colony's largest general supplying and mercantile business outside St. John's." The company was involved in shipping, shipbuilding and sealing, as well as other ventures. So important did the Munn empire become that people began to refer to Harbour Grace as "Munnsborough."

Above all, the Munn firm became known for its high-quality seal oil. *Chafe's Sealing Book* records that "Messrs' Punton and Munn's brand of Steam-Refined Pale Seal Oil was the standard on all foreign markets." Hon. Stephen Rendell of Job Brothers in St. John's wrote to Munn, asking for the secret by which they got the oil "so pale and free from smell." We don't know if Munn ever revealed the secret.

Then there's the story of jolly Irishman John Murphy, a sealing captain from Harbour Grace who couldn't read or write. Unable to remember the names of the various ropes in his ship's rigging, Murphy had coloured rags tied to the ropes. He'd call out orders like: "Pull the red rag!", "Let go the white rag!", "Hoist the green rag!" It was customary for a ship returning from the seal hunt to sail into port with all flags flying and the men firing guns. As Murphy and his men steamed into Harbour Grace in the 100-ton William, Murphy called to his gunners as the ship passed different landmarks: "Shoot the chapel!", "Shoot Ridley's!" (Murphy's suppliers). On sailing past his own house, he called out: "Shoot my wife!"

It is hard to talk about the seal hunt without making

some reference to Harbour Grace and the men and ships that sailed from this old port. In 1861, for example, Captain Nicholas Hanrahan brought in 11,000 seals in the brig Glengarry, the biggest haul of seals ever taken by a Newfoundland sailing vessel. Captain Henry Thomey sailed out of Harbour Grace to the seal hunt in the same square-rigger for thirty consecutive years. He later skippered two other ships at the seal hunt and retired without ever having lost a man or a ship, no mean feat in rough seas, grinding ice and foul weather.

With the fishery shut down, the main employer at Harbour Grace these days is a footwear factory, which has built a solid reputation for its durable working boots. It's true that Harbour Grace has seen brighter days, but the community continues to survive, adding more pages to its colourful history.

CATALINA AND PORT UNION:
Old and New

The northern side of Trinity Bay is punctuated by quite a few towns redolent with the lure of history, sometimes well-preserved, sometimes not so well preserved. Two such towns are Catalina and Port Union – the former old, the latter new – tucked into a cozy anchorage just a few miles from Bonavista. Both of these towns have their own individual stories to tell.

The history of Catalina stretches back to 1499, just two years after John Cabot touched land at Cape Bonavista. In that year, the same firm which bankrolled Cabot's voyage dispatched a fleet of twenty ships to the New World. We are told that the convoy reached Cape Bonavista on June 21 and the leader, Captain Hawkins, assigned members of his crew to look after different areas of the Newfoundland coast.

At Catalina, Hawkins sent John Sheppard ashore to represent the Queen of England, maintain law and order and build houses. Before long, to escape the oppressive hand of the fishing admirals, Sheppard moved to East (or Sheppard's) Point, now part of the community of

Catalina. Descendants of John Sheppard still live in the town, alongside heirs of other early settlers like the Manuels, Whites and Eddys.

The port of Catalina was known as Havre Sainte-Katherine (St. Catherine's Haven) when ice forced French explorer Jacques Cartier to seek shelter here nearly 500 years ago. Later, the Spanish called the port Cataluna, a name which has undergone only a minor change to its present form.

Eventually, the British captains decided to set up their headquarters in the sheltered harbour of Catalina. The Portuguese, too, had their eyes on the rich fishing grounds off the Newfoundland coast. In fact, at one point, Portuguese explorer Gaspar Corte Real sailed into the harbour at Catalina and told the English captain there that the King of Portugal had appointed him (Corte Real) Governor of Terra Nova (the Spanish name for Newfoundland). Of course, the English weren't willing to give up their claim to this profitable territory, so they reached an amicable agreement with the Portuguese to share certain ports and barter various goods.

In 1583, some of Sir Humphrey Gilbert's men found what they thought was gold in a cove not far from Catalina. They loaded some of the valuable-looking stone aboard their ship and took it back to England for analysis. The ore turned out to be iron pyrite, also known as fool's gold, which, in many parts of Newfoundland, is still called Catalina Stone. Newfoundland historians Lewis Amadeus Anspach and Richard Bonnycastle both reported that the stone on the cliff at Catalina ignited spontaneously.

By the latter part of the sixteenth century, Catalina was a popular port of call for fishermen from different European countries. By 1580, the town had a permanent population of a hundred people. Today, around 1,200 people live at Catalina, while Port Union is home to some 800.

The sea, with all its profits and perils, figures prominently in the history of Catalina. The year 1774, for instance, has been called "the year of the great storm" as well as "starvation year". To compound the hardships created by the savage storm that year, the New England colonies were refusing to trade with Newfoundland. This meant that the people of Catalina had no wheat flour, no salt pork and no salt beef, only corn meal, which, we're told, is not the tastiest food.

As with many Newfoundland communities, the seal hunt played an important role in the life of Catalina and Port Union. In March of 1853, for example, 815 men

Port Union   Calvin Coish

sailed from Catalina, headed for the ice floes off Newfoundland in search of seals. Captain Morrissey Johnson, who went from sealing to politics, hails from Catalina.

Other kinds of fish have been brought ashore here too. In 1877, a giant squid or cuttlefish washed ashore at Catalina. Two of its tentacles measured thirty feet long and were from five to eight feet thick. The huge fish was placed on display in St. John's and was later featured in the *Canadian Illustrated News*. The New York Aquarium purchased the specimen and later used it as the prototype for a model squid for the American Museum of Natural History in New York City.

Catalina was a busy port during the golden days of the Banks fishery earlier in this century. The 100-ton ships which fished out of here carried eight dories and twenty crewmen. The Labrador fishery also did much to boost the economy of this area of Newfoundland for many years. Shipbuilding, too, was a vital part of the economy.

On the cultural front, it is worth noting that Catalina was the first Newfoundland community outside St. John's to open a public library, thanks to the generosity of onetime resident Joseph Clouter, who donated 5,000 volumes to the town in 1937. The Newfoundland Public Libraries Board put money into the venture, which thrived and helped spur the expansion of library services throughout the island.

Until the cod moratorium hit Newfoundland, it was fish that kept Catalina and Port Union and their neighbours economically prosperous. The Fishery Products plant at Port Union was the province's most northerly year-round fish plant. Built in 1957 to serve inshore fishermen, in the early 1970s the plant went into year-round operation, supplied with fish from a fleet of trawlers. At one time, the plant employed more than 1,000 people from communities throughout the area.

Port Union is a much newer town than Catalina. As the name suggests, the town's beginnings are closely linked to the founding of the union movement in Newfoundland. Sir William Ford Coaker started this community in 1913 and, three years later, formed the Fishermen's Union Trading Company, which served as the lifeblood of this town for more than sixty years, before it went into receivership in 1977. From his union headquarters at Port Union, Coaker published a feisty newspaper, *The Fishermen's Advocate*. Even though his name was later tainted by talk of corruption, Coaker still

Coaker's House at Port Union   Calvin Coish

remains a hero in the eyes of many Newfoundlanders. A bust of this champion of the working man stares out from atop his towering tomb at Port Union.

These two dissimilar twin towns offer a glimpse of the essence of the Newfoundland way of life. History practically seeps from every board and brick and boulder. For this is the land of Cabot and Cartier and Corte Real and Coaker.

THE NEWFOUNDLAND RAILWAY:
Gone But Not Forgotten

It's been said that Newfoundland has the best road network for ATVs and snowmobiles in all of Canada. The road is the bed of crushed stone left behind after Canadian National shut down the railway. The iron rails have been lifted and shipped off to such faraway places as Australia and South America. In return for eliminating the Newfoundland railway, the federal government promised to give the province some $800 million for highway upgrading over a fifteen-year period.

As early as 1865, Sir Sandford Fleming included Newfoundland in his proposed All-Red Route, intended to make it possible for British subjects to travel anywhere without ever losing sight of land over which the Union Jack waved. Fifteen years later, Governor William Whiteway proposed to link St. John's by rail to the isolated outports of Notre Dame Bay. In 1881, an American consortium started work at St. John's and, that year, laid twenty miles of roadbed and ten miles of narrow-guage track. But not everyone liked the idea of a railway across Newfoundland. When surveyors reached

Foxtrap, a few miles from St. John's, they were attacked by angry women armed with brooms, pitchforks and pickled water.

The American builders found the going through harsh terrain so tough that they gave up in despair. British backers of the project then suggested a re-routed line to Harbour Grace. That line was completed in 1884, with a sailor from HMS Bacchante driving home the last spike. That sailor later became King George V of England.

When the company in charge of building the railway ran into financial trouble and folded, the Newfoundland government took over the project. On October 2, 1888, a line to Placentia was opened. But the work turned out to be so costly that the Newfoundland government decided to call tenders for future railway construction.

Robert G. Reid of Montreal made a successful bid on a rail line to Hall's Bay. By 1893, workers had reached Norris Arm, near the mouth of the Exploits River. Reid, a venturesome Scot, did the work at a cost of $15,600 per mile, with the understanding that he would forfeit $250,000 if the work wasn't completed within five years.

The Reid company continued to extend the railway and, by 1894, had passed Corner Brook, on the west coast of Newfoundland. Two years later, the Newfoundland Railway extended all the way from St. John's to its western terminus at Port aux Basques. The Reid company had taken a big gamble and reportedly lost six million dollars in the process, but Newfoundlanders had gained a railway.

In 1898, a new contract more favourable to the Reid interests was signed, giving the company control of the railway and the coastal shipping service; in 1904, the Reids were given the telegraph service. In addition, the Newfoundland government handed over generous land concessions.

The Newfoundland Railway did much to unite the communities strung across this island and allowed Joey Smallwood to spread his message promoting Confederation with Canada back in the late 1940s. It also opened up jobs "in the lumber woods" for thousands of men from outports all over this province. Some took the train, others made the trek toward the interior on foot, but, either way, the iron rails provided their route to stable employment. Every spring for many years, the railway carried hundreds of Newfoundland men to St. John's or Port aux Basques to sign up for a voyage to the ice in search of seals.

Many a Newfoundlander can recall memories of being stranded on the train in a blinding snowstorm in some

The last official train   Ron Ennis, The Advertiser

remote spot like the Gaff Topsails, deep in the heart of Newfoundland's high country. In February, 1903, for instance, an "express" train was stranded in the Gaffs for seventeen days, while the snow piled up as high as twenty-three feet in places. The weather was bitterly cold, with the temperature dropping to twenty-three below zero Celsius. In such weather conditions, it wasn't easy to find men willing to clear a blocked train. "The labourers were offered as much as thirty cents an hour," one newspaper reported, "but not enough of them could be mustered to do any appreciable work. Even the section men preferred to give up their jobs rather than work."

There are those who say the Terms of Union with Canada in 1949 guaranteed this province the services of a railway in perpetuity. Yet, despite that agreement, on July 2, 1969, the last passenger train left Port aux Basques, bound for St. John's with 350 passengers on board. That day, T*he Evening Telegram* reported that "A horde of youngsters beseiged the train at Bishop's Falls, begging for placemats, menus, and anything else that wasn't nailed down, for souvenirs ... Even as night fell, there were cars parked anywhere the highway intersected the railroad track and drivers tooted their horns in salute."

George Robertson worked for the railway for forty-five years and four months. He started as a student fireman and worked his way up to engineer. "When they took off the passenger train, you could see the thing going backwards fast," he told me. Mr. Robertson came to live in the central Newfoundland town of Bishop's Falls in 1948, when it was "a pretty little boom town." Of the railway's demise, Mr. Robertson said, "I felt very sad about the whole thing. I grew up with the railway and went to work on a hand-fired coalburner. His grandfather, father and five brothers were all railroaders.

Robertson said "the Newfoundland Railway management made the railway pay in the early 1940s. It was the biggest mode of transportation in Newfoundland at the time. I still think you can haul freight cheaper by rail than by road. They were told that in Ottawa a few years ago."

Ron Hannon is the epitome of the hardy railroad man – heavyset, friendly, and eager to talk about his life on the rails. He went to work with the Newfoundland Railway on July 13, 1948; he retired early in October, 1988, just six months before he was to retire anyway. "I still can't believe it's gone," Mr. Hannon told me. "I enjoyed it right to the last minute." Hannon's father and three brothers also worked with the railway. "Steam engines were hard work on everybody," said Mr. Hannon. "Before the days of radio communication from one end of the train to the other, it was hard work to relay communications back and forth in all kinds of weather." In fact, sending signals the length of the train often meant standing on top of the train no matter what the weather conditions."

"Before Confederation, the rolling stock was small – twenty to twenty-five tons," said Mr. Hannon. Then, with Confederation in 1949 came "the mainland stuff", weighing forty or fifty tons a piece.

In the 1950s, with diesels taking over from coal-burning steam engines, most of the work on the trains became easier and cleaner, but some of the hazards remained. Like derailments, such as the one which happened in 1986 near the Gaff Topsails. Hannon and the crew received instructions to get the plow and head for the Gaff to get the train back on the track. At one point, they decided to hook six engines together to make the climb over the hill easier. Four engines slid off the track on one side and the plow slipped off on the other side. It took four days to get everything back on the rails again.

George Saunders didn't work with the railway, but his father did. Saunders, former Mayor of Bishop's Falls, was sorry to see the railway go and fought like the dickens to keep it. "When I grew up, Bishop's Falls was alive with the railway," said Saunders. "I grew up on Station Road, fifty feet from the tracks and the yard, and it was hustle and bustle twenty-four hours a day, seven days a week, trains coming and going, hauling everything from freight to passengers to wood. My father worked with them. He gave his life to the railway. Most of the men I knew were railroaders. I went to school with railroaders' children; we were all railroading people. Those were good times to grow up. We met people from all over Newfoundland because of the railway."

At one time, between 300 and 400 people worked for the railway in Bishop's Falls. There was a staff house for crews from other communities, like Clarenville and Corner Brook.

George Saunders said the train gave people in his town "the only opportunity to see a strange face. It was a big delight for Newfoundlanders to be able to see strangers. A lot of passengers would get off here. Our town was a lot happier. The train had such a special meaning." Saunders also said he'll "never forget the breakfast of bacon and eggs" served on the train.

Gordon Lannon of Bishop's Falls worked with the Newfoundland Railway from 1944 to 1985. He went to work as a brakeman, then worked his way up to conductor on both freight and passenger trains. Starting out, Lannon earned eighty-five dollars a month, getting an extra five dollars every twelve months, until he was making the grand sum of one hundred dollars a month. Lannon says the railway deteriorated after Confederation with Canada. "I don't feel good about it," Mr. Lannon said of the railway's decline. "I don't think the railway should ever have gone the way it did, with the roads for rails deal. We should have waited four or five years to build up the roads. If the railway had been maintained the way it should have been, it would never have shut down."

I have my own memories of the renowned Newfie Bullet, some pleasant, some not so pleasant. I remember waiting for hours at Notre Dame Junction, then boarding the train at two or three o'clock in the morning, a mere three or four hours behind schedule, then heading back to St. John's. I remember the endless ride, the conductor weaving among the noisy passengers, calling out "Next stop, Gambo," "Next stop, Alexander Bay Station," "Next stop, Terra Nova," the sweaty card players slipping their poker money out of sight as the conductor passed bay. I remember standing on the platform between cars to catch a breath of fresh air, and the train raucously announcing its arrival as it rattled and roared into the old city just after daybreak.

THE COLONIAL BUILDING:
If These Walls Could Talk

Some years ago I read a newspaper account which reported that the Colonial Building in St. John's had been hit by lightning. That probably wasn't the first such strike and it certainly wasn't the most newsworthy thing the building has witnessed. For 110 years, the grand old stone structure was the seat of the Newfoundland government and the scene of more than one scuffle.

In the early 1800s, the Newfoundland government was having a hard time finding a place to meet. On December 26, 1832, they set themselves up in a former tavern and lodging house. When he opened Parliament on January 1, 1833, Governor Cochrane announced that, "A temporary accommodation has been provided in which to hold your sittings. It does not afford all the conveniences I could have wished for, but I trust will be found to answer that purpose during the present session." That first session of the Newfoundland Parliament opened to the boom of a nineteen-gun salute from Fort William.

On July 26, 1833, the House heard a petition from Mrs. Travers, asking that government pay the rent they owed for using her house. For whatever reason, the petition was ignored and Mrs. Travers was forced to continue waiting for payment of the rent. Frustrated in her efforts, the landlady obtained a warrant and seized the speaker's chair and desk, the cocked hat and sword of the sergeant-at-arms, and various House documents. She then put some of the articles, including the chair, desk and mace, up for sale.

Turfed out by the landlady, the government then moved into the courthouse and began attempts to get back the items Mrs. Travers had taken. The lady said she had sold some of the articles, but she eventually handed them back to the government. In 1836, Mrs. Travers

The Colonial Building Calvin Coish

COLONIAL BUILDING

finally received payment for back rent and incidental expenses.

Cramped for space at the courthouse, the Newfoundland Legislature, on April 7, 1836, proposed "that the vacant ground on Church Hill ... be secured for the purpose of erecting thereon a Colonial Building, to serve as well for the accommodation of the legislature, as for a public market house for the town of St. John's and for other purposes." The Legislative Council approved the bill on May 2.

On June 3, 1836, Governor Prescott received an application from William Haddon, an Englishman who had supervised the building of Government House, to oversee construction of the proposed seat of government. It seems that nothing further was heard of Haddon's application.

Two years later, a Mr. Kent requested in the House "an account of the proceedings of the commissioners appointed under the Act to authorize the erection of a Colonial House."

On September 1, 1838, the Governor responded: "Gentlemen, I will request the commissioners of the Colonial Building to furnish the information asked for in this address."

On September 17, the House examined the report of the commissioners. On September 28, Mr. Morris moved a resolution which read in part: "An Act for erecting a Colonial Building in the town of St. John's is inoperative for the purposes contemplated by the Legislature, owing to the insufficiency of some of the provisions of the said Act. Resolved, that an address be presented to His Excellency the Governor praying His Excellency to suspend all operations under the Act." In other words, the government wanted to call off construction of a

Colonial Building.

The resolution was adopted by the House and forwarded to Her Majesty's Council, who turned it down on the grounds that "the obvious and usual way of proceeding would be to amend the Act by a bill for that purpose."

Although detailed plans for construction of a Colonial Building were drafted by 1839, construction did not start until 1846, largely because of problems in finding a suitable location. The government finally settled on a site on Military Road, in the face of objections from Major Robe, Commanding Officer of the Royal Engineers. On June 9, 1846, the Great Fire levelled much of St. John's, including the courthouse, and the Legislature moved into the Orphan Asylum School.

On May 24, 1847, Queen Victoria's birthday, government officials gathered to lay the cornerstone for a Colonial Building, scheduled to be completed by January of the following year. But the building wasn't finished in 1838 and the government moved into other temporary quarters on Water Street.

The Colonial Building finally opened officially on January 28, 1850. Governor LeMarchant dedicated "to the future advancement and wellbeing of the country a building which from its magnificence and extent will henceforth invest our legislature with an additional degree of interest and veneration." Little did he know that the history of this building would not always be smooth.

It wasn't long before something happened. Around December 1, 1850, as *The Newfoundlander* later reported, "the office of the Colonial Treasurer in the Colonial Building was broken into and the chest of the Savings Bank robbed of 413 pounds ... The Government has offered a reward of 100 pounds and free pardon to an accomplice for the discovery of the perpetrators; but no clue has yet been given." Two men were arrested three and a half months later.

Many times this old building echoed to the chatter, laughter and dancing of fancy balls, such as the one held on July 25, 1852 for the crews of three British warships visiting St. John's. *The Newfoundlander* reported that "The Assembly was composed of nearly all the ladies and gentlemen of the garrison, and the civil departments of the Government, the officers of the three men-of-war in port, and the elite of beauty, rank and respectability of the town."

An August 10, 1858 gala at Colonial Building celebrated the successful landing of the Atlantic Cable at Bay Bulls Arm, Trinity Bay. A ball of July 25, 1860 marked the visit of the Prince of Wales, who later became King Edward VII. On that occasion, the building was decorated with pink and white calico, flags, evergreen boughs and artificial flowers. The menu included "all procurable delicacies from New York and such wines including best claret and twelve dozen of champagne." Each evening during the Prince's visit, a dazzling fireworks display was set off from the roof of the Colonial Building.

1887 was Queen Victoria's Jubilee Year and, on August 11, the elite of St. John's celebrated with a ball at the Colonial Building. The following day *The Evening Telegram* headlined its coverage "The Breakdown at the Colonial" and called the event "a Bacchanalian spree on money stolen from the treasury of the Commonwealth." *The Telegram* also said "The affair was a failure (and) ... the attendance was comparatively small, and consisted for the most part of people who are willing to go anywhere and do anything for a night's enjoyment, without caring two straws where the money comes from or who pays the piper." On the other hand, *The Royal Gazette* said the ball had been " a brilliant success".

There's an interesting postscript to that ball of 1887. In preparation for the dance, the organizers removed the carpet from the floor and placed it in an adjoining room. Sometime after the ball, the carpet was reported missing. Some years later, historian Maurice Devine unlocked the secret and reported in a local paper that "One of the officials of the House, long since gone to a better world, locked the carpet up in a certain room in the basement of the Assembly and confided the secret of its whereabouts to only one other man. The latter was promised a good slice of the carpet later on, but he found out that the principal in the game meant to deceive him, so he decided on boldly lifting it from the lifter. He confided his intention to a carman who was hauling birch billets to the public offices, and this latter, one evening in broad daylight, drove out through the gate of the Colonial Building with presumably an empty dry goods case on his cart (in which he used to bring the birch billets) but in which was snugly tucked away the Assembly carpet. The name of the man who got the carpet has never been known to more than three persons from that day till this, and wild horses will never tear the secret from me."

The Colonial Building was the scene of several fracases and fusses. Like the riot of 1861, which happened during the first sitting of the Hoyles Government. The dispute started when the government decided to reject Messrs. Hogsett and Furey as members for the district of Harbour Main. An angry mob gathered outside the building to protest the government's decision. The government called in soldiers and, in the resulting melee, three people were killed.

In 1886, there was another riot when an irate gang crashed through windows and charged into the House, demanding jobs on construction of the Newfoundland Railway. Sir Ambrose Shea led the crowd outside and promised that their demands would be met. Later, police arrested several men involved in that dispute.

On April 5, 1932, calling for action on rumours of government corruption, an angry crowd marched from the Majestic Theatre to the Colonial Building, where they smashed doors and windows and trashed the place. *The Evening Telegram* later reported that "Typewriters, bookcases, books, and documents, as well as chairs and tables were flung into the ground and the scene this morning is likened to that of a gigantic explosion within the precincts of the Colonial Building. Every pane of glass on all four sides of the structure was broken as well as those in the doors and corridors. Large stones were flung into the Assembly and the Legislature Council room." Total damages were estimated at $10,000.

Then there's the story of how the delicate frescoes came to be painted on the ceilings of the Colonial Building (and Government House). The paintings were done by Alexander Pindikowski, a Pole who had been found guilty of passing forged cheques. He was sentenced to fifteen months in prison; after serving his sentence he was to leave the country. The government, aware of Pindikowski's reputation as a fresco artist, put him to work painting the ceilings. Pindikowski did such a good job that a month was taken off his sentence. And it seems he never did leave the country, for in 1882 he was advertising his artistic talents in a local paper.

The final session of the Newfoundland Assembly

under Responsible Government was held on December 2, 1933. The next year, Newfoundland went from being a self-governing dominion to a colony administered by a commission of government. But the new colonial government never did meet in the Colonial Building. In 1949, Newfoundland joined Canada, and the first session of the new province's first parliament began in the old building on July 13, 1949.

On June 25, 1956, Premier J. R. Smallwood officially turned on the illuminated fountain in front of the Colonial Building. For fifteen years or so, the fountain was a popular attraction.

The Newfoundland Government met at the Colonial Building for a final farewell to the old place on July 28, 1959. Since then, Confederation Building, on a hill overlooking the city, has been the seat of government. No matter how elaborate and fancy that structure is, with all its assorted wings and additions, it will have a hard time matching the colourful history of the simple, old stone building which now houses the Newfoundland Archives.

BURIN:
Between Past and Present

Smalltown Newfoundland. It could be any one of dozens of small communities dotting this province's coastline. Population under 3,000. More than 200 years old. Incorporated in 1950. But this town, or rather, collection of little villages, is as captivating and unique as any other community. In short, as Harold Horwood wrote in his book *Newfoundland*, we're talking about a "collection of pocket-edition villages that add up to bright but discontented Burin."

Situated close to the heel of the boot-shaped Burin Peninsula kicking out into the Atlantic just a few miles from the French islands of St. Pierre and Miquelon, Burin is being tugged toward the twenty-first century, while being reminded of its rich history.

The name Burin reportedly comes from burine, a French word for a kind of engraving tool. The story goes that a crew member on one of the first French ships to enter the sheltered harbour was holding a burine in his hand as the ship sailed between the steep cliffs. The shape of the harbour reminded him so much of a burine that he shouted the word. The name stuck, with British settlers dropping the last letter.

One of the earliest settlements in the area was Burin Bay, at the entrance to Burin Inlet. In 1820, Burin Bay was a thriving settlement, preferred for its sheltered harbour, closeness to the fishing grounds and thick woods nearby.

The exact origins of settlement at Burin are hard to trace, but tradition holds that an Englishman by the name of Dr. Walsh, jumped a British man o' war which was patrolling the Newfoundland coast. At that time, in the early 1700s, the notorious and dreaded press gangs were on the prowl, forcing men to take up arms for the British Crown against countries like France and Spain. Not too keen on the idea of being conscripted, Walsh reportedly hid out at Burin for four years. Later he moved to nearby Great Burin, where he met the Holletts from Dorset County, England, who used to fish in Newfoundland each summer and, like many others, returned home to England before winter set in.

Apparently, Dr. Walsh persuaded the Holletts to settle at Great Burin permanently. Today, Hollett is one of the most common surnames in Burin; two of the town's mayors have had that surname. A glance through the phone book shows other typical Burin names – Drake, Brushett, Coady, Foote, Moulton, Walsh – most of them of British origin. Burin has turned out quite a few noteworthy people, including at least fifty sea captains.

Modern-day Burin comprises a dozen or so small villages, many with unusual place names – like Step-Aside, reportedly named after a small English town. Ship Cove gets its name from a shipbuilding enterprise begun in 1718 by Christopher Spurrier from Poole, England.. The Spurrier property, later taken over by the firm of C.

F. and W. Bishop, was wiped out by fire in the early 1930s. Sadly, many of the other early buildings, if not levelled by fire, were torn down. In the early days, Path End, now part of Burin, was the end of the road. The community of Salt Pond gets its common name from a body of salt water nearby.

The harbour of Great Burin is flanked on the west by the towering island of Shalloway. To protect the early settlers from French and American privateers, the British built a fort on Shalloway which came to be called The Battery. At the eastern entrance to the harbour, at Parson's Point, similar fortifications were constructed and a garrison of soldiers was stationed nearby.

Popular opinion holds that the Anglican Rectory, torn down around 1950, was the headquarters for the British garrison stationed there around 1800. Guns, cannons and an assortment of other military items have been found at several spots in the area – Man o' War Hill, Troke's Point, Paul's Hill, Jersey Room, Power's Hill and Morris's Point.

Burin was, for many years, a major port for sailors and fishermen. Foreign vessels, especially from Europe, often stopped at Burin. In April of 1812, Newfoundland Governor Duckworth reported that "In the harbour (of Burin) alone, there is generally during the eight months of the year from six to twelve sail of square-rigged vessels, and about one hundred and twenty fishing boats of various sizes, for most of which the merchants here keep a large stock of provisions, salt and every material necessary for fishing, which may be fairly estimated at 120,000 pounds."

Earlier in this century, the harbour, flanked by cliffs rising steeply to 400 feet in places, would practically come alive with dozens of Lunenberg bankers, complete with sails, putting up there overnight. The famed Bluenose, captained by Angus Walters, called in at Burin many times throughout its illustrious career.

In 1942, Fishery Products secured the industrial base of present-day Burin, when the company opened a fish-processing plant at Burin North. Later, when a new plant was built, local inshore fishermen and bankers couldn't keep up with the plant's demand for fish, so side trawlers, later replaced by stern trawlers, with local crews, provided a steady supply of fish. The Burin fish plant used to employ 400 people, while another 150 men worked on trawlers at sea. But that's all changed with the ban on codfishing, and it's hard to say if things will ever be the way they were.

In a province which is no stranger to sea tragedies, Burin has seen more than a few. One story dates back to 1857, when the Swedish ship Monasco ran ashore near Burin. Most of the crew, including the captain, were rescued, while all the passengers, except for the captain's wife, drowned. Later, while exploring the underwater wreck of the Monasco, diver David Dobbin found that the doors to the passengers' cabins had been nailed shut. It seems that the captain and crew had stolen the valuables from the immigrant passengers the ship carried. We are told that the captain later left his first wife and married another woman who had been in on the conspiracy aboard the Monasco. Near Burin, Monasco Point pokes out into the sea, an indelible reminder of this eerie story.

On July 20, 1894, the White Star liner Majestic ran into the fishing schooner Antelope from Burin. Captain Bugden and most of the Antelope's crew were rescued, but two men died – one by drowning, the other from injuries received in the collision.

The most devastating tragedy ever to hit Burin happened in 1929. On Monday, November 18 of that year, an earthquake far out under the Atlantic pushed a fifty-foot-high wave of water surging toward the sleeping inhabitants of the south coast of Newfoundland. Twenty-seven people, including nine at Burin, lost their lives in the maelstrom.

Like those all over Newfoundland, the people of Burin often had to come up with their own forms of recreation and amusement. One rather unusual game, which seems to have been unique to the Burin Peninsula, was called Fiona, after a government revenue ship, which intercepted other ships returning from St. Pierre to check their cargoes and levy taxes or, on a bonus day, uncover a load of illicit rum. The game Fiona was played on ice, with different points being named after places near Burin, with another point being St. Pierre. The object of the game was to get from St. Pierre to any point on the Burin Peninsula without getting snagged by the Fiona.

According to early records, organized education in the Burin area began around 1836. Later, in 1863, the Irish Sisters of Mercy started a school there. Today, the area has some of the most modern schools in Newfoundland.

The move to bring together the assortment of little communities near Burin really started in 1945 with the formation of a community council. In 1950, the town was incorporated, uniting the communities of Burin Bay, Ship Cove – Path End, Ship Cove Proper and Burin North. Modern-day Burin also includes Collins' Cove, Kirby's Cove, Bull's Cove, Long Cove, Little Salmonier, Burin Bay Arm and Salt Pond, as well as several new subdivisions.